World's Greatest
ARTISTS

Wonder
House

(An imprint of Prakash Books)

Wonder House

(An imprint of Prakash Books)

contact@wonderhousebooks.com

ISBN : 9789388369053

CONTENTS

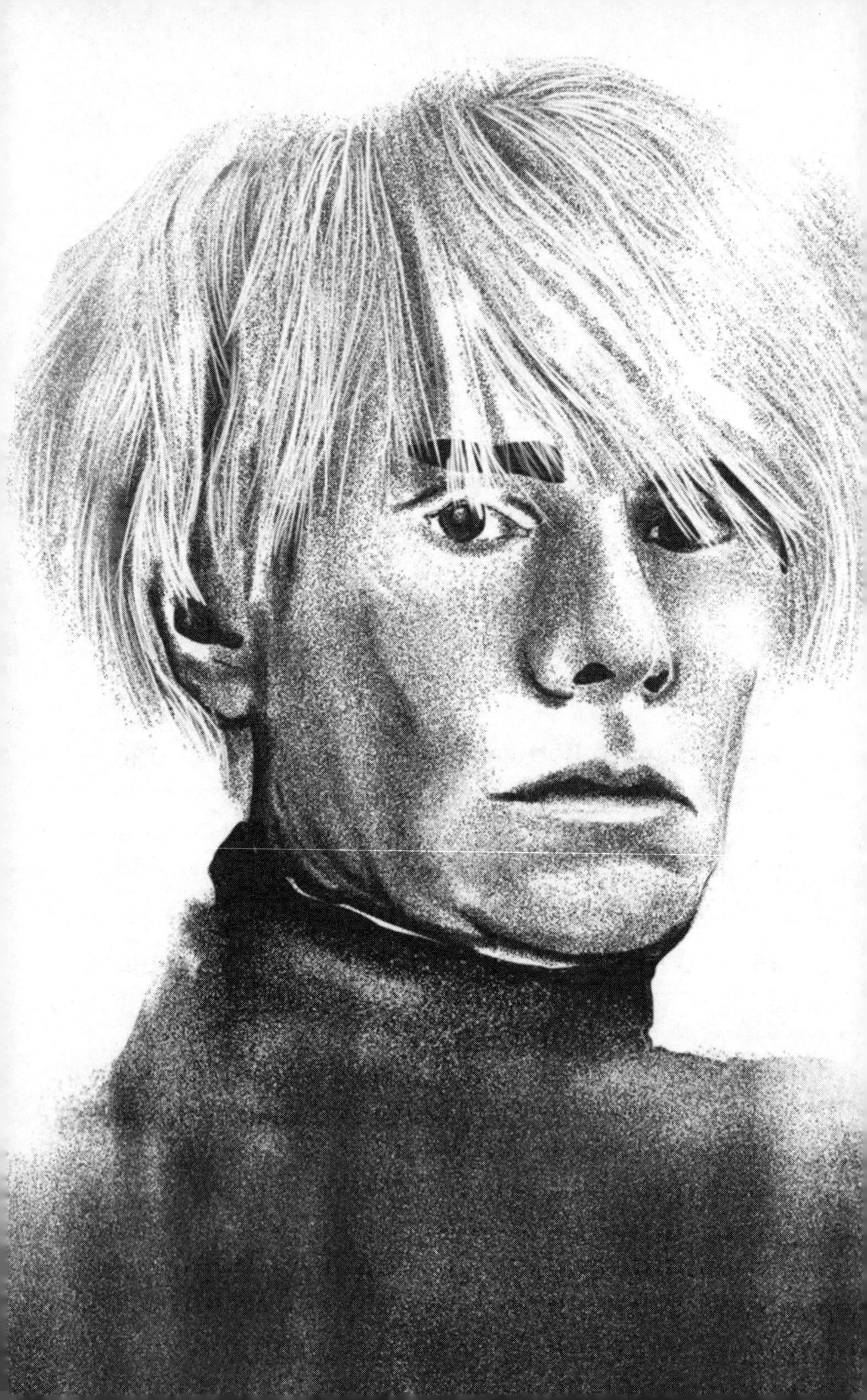

ANDY WARHOL

BIRTH: *August 6, 1928*
Pittsburgh, Pennsylvania, USA

DEATH: *February 22, 1987 (aged 58)*
New York City, USA

A ndy Warhol was an American artist and filmmaker. He was the first one to introduce a new form of art called pop art and the pop art movement of the 1960s. His famous works use renderings of Coca-Cola bottles and tins of Campbell Soup as a commentary on increasing materialism and capitalism.

Andy Warhol's full name was Andrew Warhola. He was born on August 6, 1928, in Pittsburgh, Pennsylvania, to Julia and Ondrej Warhola. He had two elder brothers. His father was a construction worker and his mother was an embroiderer and an artist. Andy was a weak child and suffered from many health disorders. At a very early age, he suffered from a neurological disorder, Sydenham chorea that led to frequent trips to the hospital. Andy was a loner and had no friends due to his poor health and absence from school. He graduated from Schenley High School in 1945, at the young age of 16.

His mother then taught him how to draw. He soon developed an interest in painting, photography and movies. He lost his father when he was just a teenager. His father had always supported him and had even saved money for his college education. He attended the Carnegie Institute of Technology and pursued a bachelor's degree in fine arts. He was the first one in his family who studied beyond high school. He then graduated from art school with a degree in pictorial design, which later helped him develop his new art form.

In his college days, he honed his skills as an illustrator. He was introduced to the world of high fashion, which later led to his interest in becoming an illustrator. During his summer break, he worked at a department store and created window displays. After he graduated from college, Andy and his artist friend, Philip Pearlstein, moved to New York City. There, both of them continued to explore the world of art.

His first job as an artist was in advertising and magazines. He worked as an illustrator. He gained lots of attention for his ink drawings for shoe advertisements. In just a few years, he became a successful commercial artist. During one of his jobs, Andy's name in the credits was misspelt as "Warhol" instead of "Warhola". He decided to keep the name for his future artworks. He was also offered a deal with RCA Records. Andy designed various album covers for the label. He was one of the artists who adopted the 'Silk Screen' printmaking process in the 1950s.

During the 1950s, he received many illustration projects from major fashion magazines like *Glamour, Vogue,* and *Harper's Bazaar.* He introduced the blotted line technique. It caught the eyes of many art directors. He also worked for I. Miller, a popular shoe company. His jobs in the advertisement world helped him to venture into the art world.

In the 1960s, he tried his luck and got into fine arts. Andy bought a four-storey building from the money he'd earned from his previous jobs. He used to try his art on the walls of his home. Andy's art was unique at the time. He called them Pop paintings and these paintings had a somewhat unfinished look to them. Over time, he evolved his style into something more flat and graphic. He combined art with everyday objects. And this made him famous.

It was 1961 when Andy introduced the concept of using mass-produced commercial goods in his art. He called it Pop Art. He used images and reproduced them over and over for same products. He made pop art for different kinds of objects like electric chairs, Campbell's soup cans and Coca-Cola bottles. His art for Campbell's soup gained him lots of attention all over the world. He did the same for famous people such as Marilyn Monroe, Elizabeth Taylor and more. He repeated the same picture over and over again, but used different colors and effects in every picture. Soon, Andy founded his own studio named The Factory in New York. He was also a great filmmaker. He made hundreds of films such as *Sleep, Empire,* and *Eat.* His major work as a filmmaker was *Chelsea Girls.* It was his first commercial success.

He was successful in other areas of art as well. His world famous piece was a portrait of the Chinese Communist leader Mao Zedong. He even helped found the New York Academy of Art for aspiring artists. In 1979, he was hired by the automobile company, BMW. They wanted Andy to paint their new model, super-car BMW M1. He also exhibited his collection named 'The Jewish Geniuses', which became a great success. He received awards and honors throughout his life. The US Postal Service issued a stamp as a tribute to Andy Warhol's achievements. Warhol died on February 22, 1987, in a New York hospital, at the age of 59.

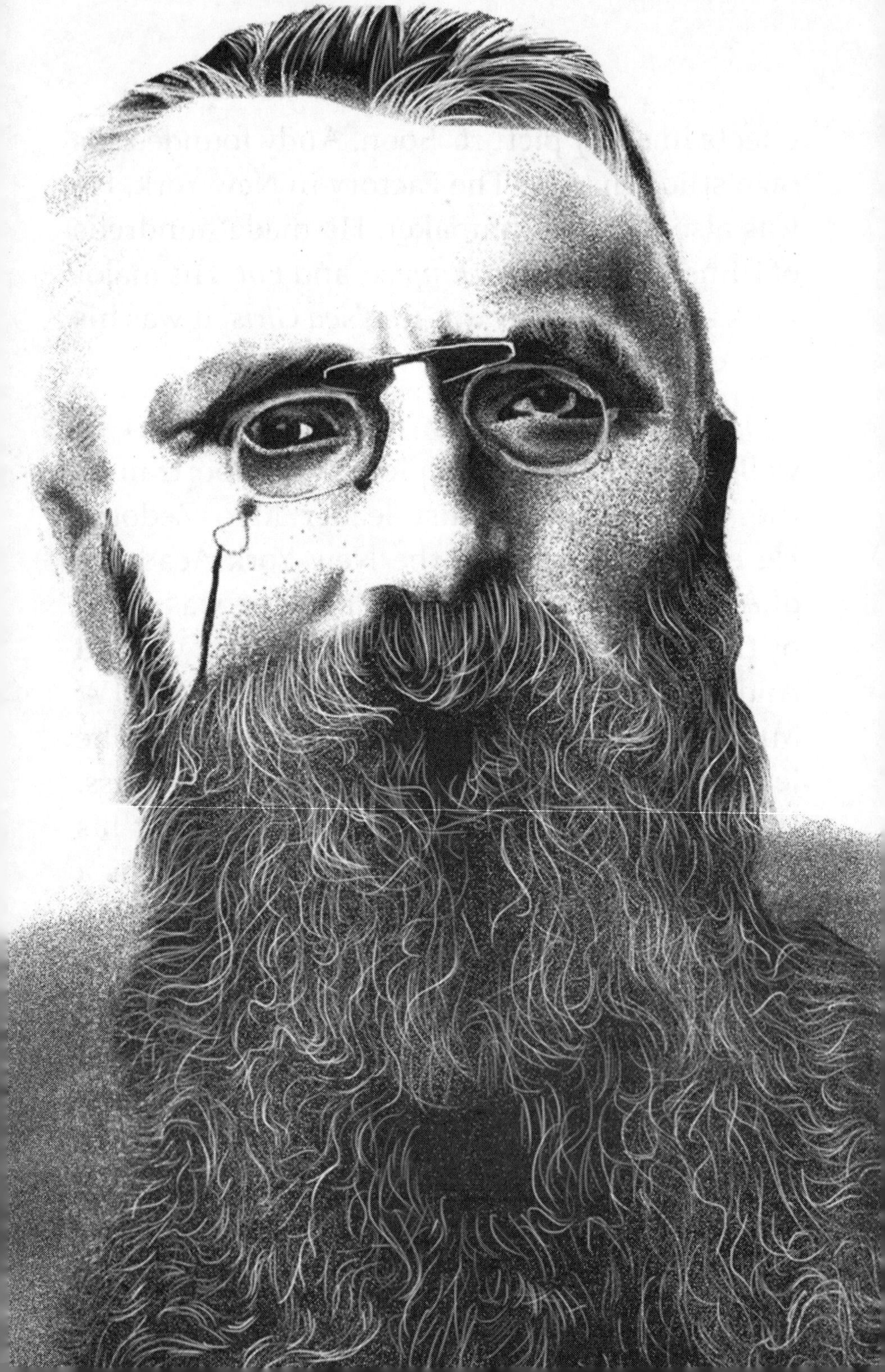

AUGUSTE RODIN

✦❧❦❧✦

BIRTH: November 12, 1840
Paris, France

DEATH: November 17, 1917 (aged 77)
Meudon, France

Auguste Rodin was a French sculptor, illustrator and painter. He was the creator of beautiful world-famous bronze and marble figures. He is considered to be one of the greatest portraitists in the history of sculpture. Rodin's most famous artworks include *'The Thinker'* and *'The Kiss'*.

Auguste Rodin's full name was François-Auguste-René Rodin. He was born in Paris, France, in 1840. He attended a boarding school which was run by his uncle. But he left it in 1854. After that, he went to an art school called Petite

École. There, he studied art and mathematics. In his early days, he experimented with drawing and modeling with clay. Later, he also applied to France's prestigious art school, Ecole des Beaux-Arts, but was rejected.

He did odd jobs to support his family. Along with his jobs, he continued to practice art. In 1858, he started to work in an art workshop. There, he developed his sculpting skills. One of his pieces from that time was a sculpture of a man with a broken nose. Rodin faced many rejections in his life. He submitted his first major work, *'Mask of the Man with the Broken Nose'*, to the Salon, an art exhibition. The piece was rejected because it represented the face of a servant and ignored traditional ideals of beauty.

His next work was *'The Age of Bronze'*. It was his most talked-about piece in Parisian society. Rodin got the inspiration for the *'Age of Bronze'* from Michelangelo's *'Dying Slave'*. He always appreciated Michelangelo's art and how he showed human form in his work. Rodin tried to attempt the same and combined his own ideas on human nature for this statue. As a result, throughout his career, Rodin was associated with and compared to Michelangelo.

In 1877, he traveled to France studied Gothic cathedrals, and researched the architectural features and observations of the Gothic style. In 1879, he worked in a porcelain factory. He also received a new project called *'The Gates of Hell'*. This work was commissioned by the French Ministry of Fine Arts. He took the inspiration for this masterpiece from the 12th-century epic poem *The Divine Comedy,* by Dante and from *The Flowers of Evil* by Charles Baudelaire, published around 1857. However, he died before finishing it.

Rodin's most famous works were influenced by some of the great artists of Parisian society including the writers Victor Hugo and Honore de Balzac, and the artist Claude Lorrain. His other major artworks include *'The Kiss'*, *'Ugolino'*, *'Adam'*, *'Eve'* and *'The Thinker'*, which were all his independent works. In 1889, he created a sculpture of Victor Hugo for the Pantheon and a statue of Claude Lorraine.

In 1894, Rodin moved to Meudon and participated in many exhibitions. In 1900, he participated in the World Exhibition in Paris, in which he displayed hundreds of his works. He established himself as an artist here. He also received honorary doctorates from the Universities of Glasgow and Oxford.

The significant factor contributing to Rodin's success as a portraitist was that he continued to work on his skills throughout his life. His works were marked greatly by Realism. His work was heavily inspired by Donatello and other great sculptors of the Renaissance. He also experimented with different techniques. He made *'The Gates of Hell'* using several hundred pieces. His later works were more expressionist, such as the *'Monument to Balzac'*.

In his later years, he lived at the beautiful Hotel Biron. He was neighbors with the well-known painter, Henri Matisse; dancer, Isadora Duncan; and writer, Jean Cocteau. He used the ground floor as his studio and helped avert its destruction by entering into an agreement with the French government. The agreement required him to donate all his work to the State in return. After his death, the same hotel was converted into a museum in his honor.

Rodin remained unmarried for most of his life. He had a son with his long-term partner Rose Beuret. Later, he was in a relationship with a sculptor named Camille Claudel. Claudel was also the inspiration for Rodin's most famous work, *'The Kiss'*. But they soon separated, and Rodin married Beuret in 1917. Rodin died on November 17, 1917, in Meudon at the age of 77. His popularity had declined towards the end, but after his death, his legacy solidified. Rodin remains one of the few sculptors widely known even outside the visual arts society.

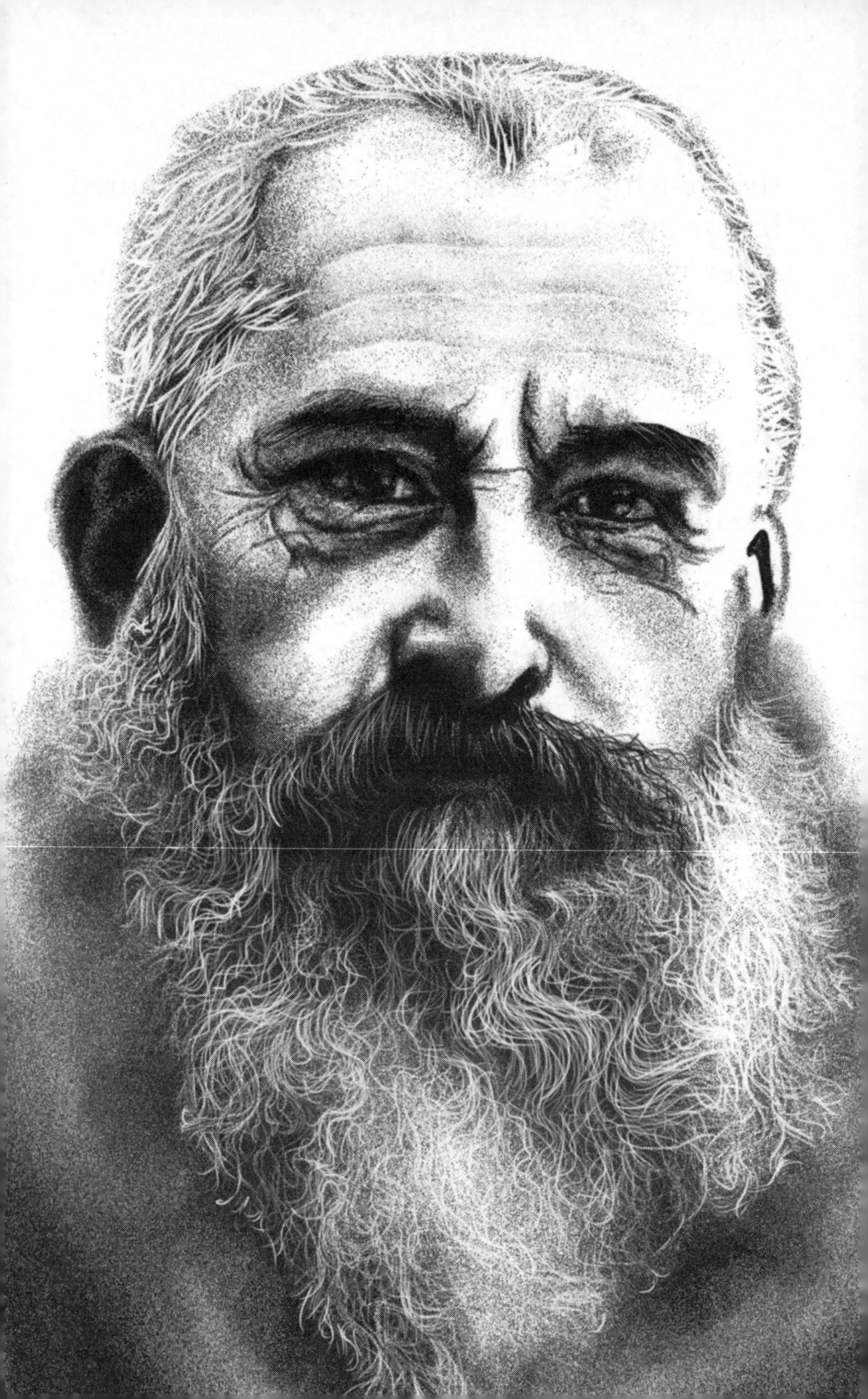

CLAUDE MONET

❦

BIRTH: November 14, 1840
Paris, France

DEATH: December 5, 1926 (aged 86)
France

Claude Monet was a famous French painter of the Impressionist period. He used to capture his daily life's best moments on his canvas. He remains one of the most well-known personalities in the field of art. One of Monet's most significant contributions was his painting style. The style was termed 'Impressionism'.

Monet's full name was Oscar-Claude Monet. Claude Monet was born on 14th November, 1840, in Paris, to Louise-Justine Aubrée Monet and Adolphe Monet. Claude was the second son born to the couple. His father was a businessman and his mother was a singer. At the age of eleven, Claude entered art school. His mother encouraged his dream of becoming an artist. However, his father wanted him to take over the family's grocery business.

Monet began to draw caricatures of famous people. As a kid, he used to sell these caricatures to earn extra money. During that time, he met amazing French artists. One of them was the renowned landscape painter Eugène Boudin. From Eugene, he learned the basic skills and technique of art. It was Eugene who introduced Monet to oil paints. He taught Monet an outdoor technique for painting. It changed his approach towards art.

Monet lost his mother when he was sixteen years old. He decided to leave school and went to live with his aunt. Monet moved to Paris and studied art at the Academie Suisse. There, he observed different artists' styles. Monet often spent his free time painting what he saw. He also met several painters who became his friends. One of them was Manet Edouard.

In 1861, he was enlisted in the army. But Monet had to quit just after two years, as he was suffering from typhoid. After resigning from the army, he became a student of Charles Gleyre in Paris. Monet also developed new methods of art; he began to use the effects of light and rapid brush strokes in his works, which later came to be known as Impressionism. Monet gained fame when two of his marine landscape paintings were selected in an annual art show.

Monet's masterpiece was called *'Camille'*. This painting was also known as the *'Woman in The Green Dress'*. It was a huge artwork, which he painted outside in the natural light. He spent a lot of time on this painting. He presented it at the Salon. It turned out to be a milestone in his career.

In 1870, Monet moved to London. During his free time, he observed the works of other artists. There, he met Paul Durand-Ruel who became his first art-dealer.

By 1871, Monet had moved to Zaandam, Netherlands. He made 25 paintings within a few months. After the Franco-Prussian war ended, Monet relocated to France. He stayed there for seven years and created some of the most significant paintings of all time. Monet also became friends with several leading artists. Together, they started the Society of Anonymous Painters, Sculptors, and Printmakers. In this society, they experimented with art instead of indulging in the same classical art that satisfied the art critics of Paris at the time. One of these paintings was *'Impression: Sunrise'* which was inspired by Le Havre harbor in the morning fog. This painting was a great example of the new style. The lighting gave the viewer the feeling that the sun had just risen. Based on the title of the painting, M. Louis Leroy tauntingly dubbed this group of artists as "Impressionists".

During the year 1883, Monet traveled to the Mediterranean, where he painted landmarks, landscapes, and seascapes. He did a remarkable series of paintings in Venice and then in London. He painted two important sets including *'The*

Views of the Parliament' and *'The Views of the Charing Cross Bridge'.*

He used light as the central theme in his art. Monet began to paint a series of similar scenes. He would paint at different times of the day and in different types of weather. He painted a series on haystacks, the Rouen Cathedral and the London Parliament.

Monet spent the last few years of his life (from 1914 to almost until his death) painting his biggest project. It was a series based on the pond by his home. It was a large painting capturing the pond in different lighting conditions in panels titled Morning, Green Reflections, The Clouds and Sunset. It took him ten years to finish and he called it *'Grandes Decorations'.*

Monet married twice and had two children. He developed cataract as he grew older and went through a series of related operations towards the end. Monet died of lung cancer on December 5, 1926, at the age of 86.

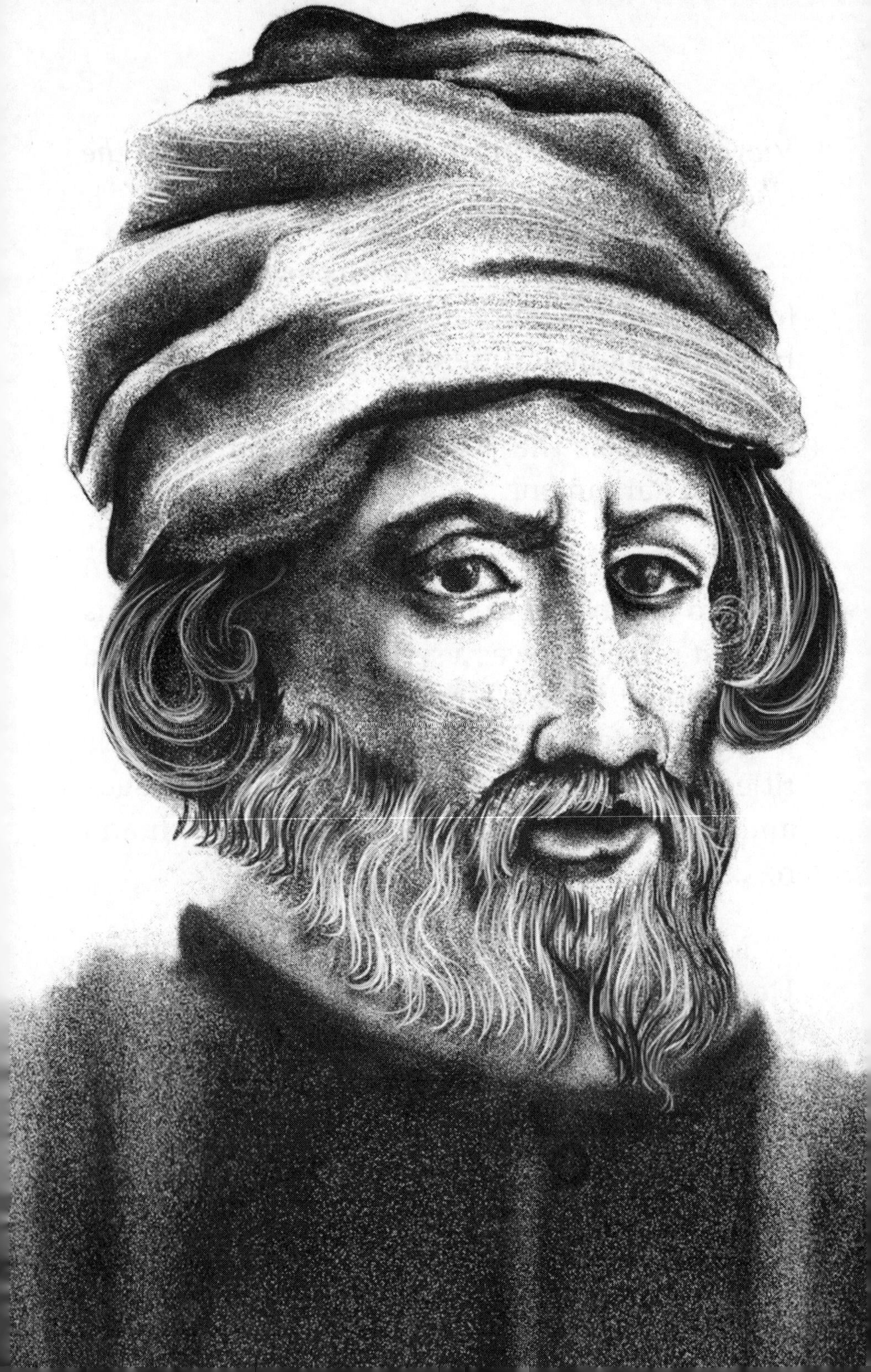

DONATELLO

BIRTH: c. 1386
Florence, Italy

DEATH: December 13, 1466
Florence, Italy

Donatello was a master of bronze and marble sculpture. He is regarded as one of the greatest Italian Renaissance artists and was recognized for his life-like sculptures. His sculptures reflected the feelings of joy and sorrow through their realistic faces and poses. His major works include the statue of David, and two outstandingly unique works, *'St Mark'* and *'St John the Evangelist'*.

Donatello's birth name was Donato di Niccolò di Betto Bardi. He was born in 1386 in Florence,

Italy, to Niccolò di Betto Bardi. His father was a member of the Guild of Wool Combers in Florence. For his education, he studied at the home of the Martellis, a famous and wealthy Florentine family of bankers and art patrons. There, he was introduced to art and sculpture. He received art training from a local goldsmith and naturally gained knowledge about metals and other substances. As a result, he began to take an interest in sculpturing.

After that, he started to work with the famous metalworker and sculptor Lorenzo Ghiberti. He learned the art of Gothic sculpturing. He assisted Ghiberti in creating the North Baptistery gates of the Florence Cathedral. The first sculpture he commissioned was in 1406. In 1408, he created a life-size marble sculpture of David, simply named 'David'. It was his one of the most famous classical works. It fascinated people because of its free-standing nature.

Donatello started to work in various goldsmiths' shops to earn money. The experience and knowledge he gained eventually changed the fifteenth-century Italian art scene.

Other popular works of Donatello were the marble sculptures *'St Mark'* placed in the Orsanmichele Church and *'St John the Evangelist'* for the cathedral in Florence. He mastered the art of making larger-than-life figures and developed amazing skills. He created five statues including the *'Beardless Prophet'*, *'Bearded Prophet'*, *'The Sacrifice of Isaac'*, *'Zuccone'*, and *'Jeremiah'*.

He met another sculptor, Michelozzo during this time, and they often collaborated. Michelozzo was famous for his architecture and Donatello for his sculptures. They also toured Rome around 1425. His time in Rome made him fall in love with ornamentation and the classical forms of arts. He worked on projects such as the tomb of Pope John XXIII and the tomb of Cardinal Brancacci. Other than that, he sculpted the statues of *'Faith'* and *'Hope'* in Siena. Their innovations in building the burial chambers later influenced many other Florentine tombs. Donatello soon met the famous Medici family.

In 1430, the Medici approached Donatello to commission his famous Bronze statue, *'David'* for the court. This bronze statue was a stepping stone in his career. The statue was a spark for the Renaissance period of art. It is considered to be the first major Renaissance sculpture. In 1443, Donatello traveled to Padua. There, he completed his other major work called *'Gattamelata'*. The statue was of Erasmo riding a horse in full battle costume. It was the first equestrian (a rider on horseback) bronze statue created since the Romans. It became a source of inspiration for other equestrian statues that were later created in Italy and Europe.

In Padua, he also created the high altar of St Antonio and seven life-sized bronze sculptures. It made him the most acclaimed sculptor. After 1443, he spent ten years as the head of a huge workshop. Donatello brought a revolutionary change around this time; he began to create statues based on illusions and space. In 1455, he returned to Florence.

He only completed two works of art, *'St John the Baptist'* and a pair of bronze doors to go with the sculpture, and an extraordinary figure of St Mary Magdalene, between 1450-1455.

Most of his unfinished pieces were

completed by his students, but they maintained the artist's signature style. Donatello soon became bedridden, which limited his work. In the last few years of his life, Donatello created several wooden sculptures. But they were not well-received as a new generation of excellent marble sculptors came about, changing the Florentine sculpting scene.

He died due to unknown reasons on December 13, 1466, in Florence, Italy. He left a great legacy as the most significant sculptor of the early Renaissance. Along with Da Vinci, Michelangelo and Shakespeare, Donatello became the focus of a movement of artists that contributed highly to European culture.

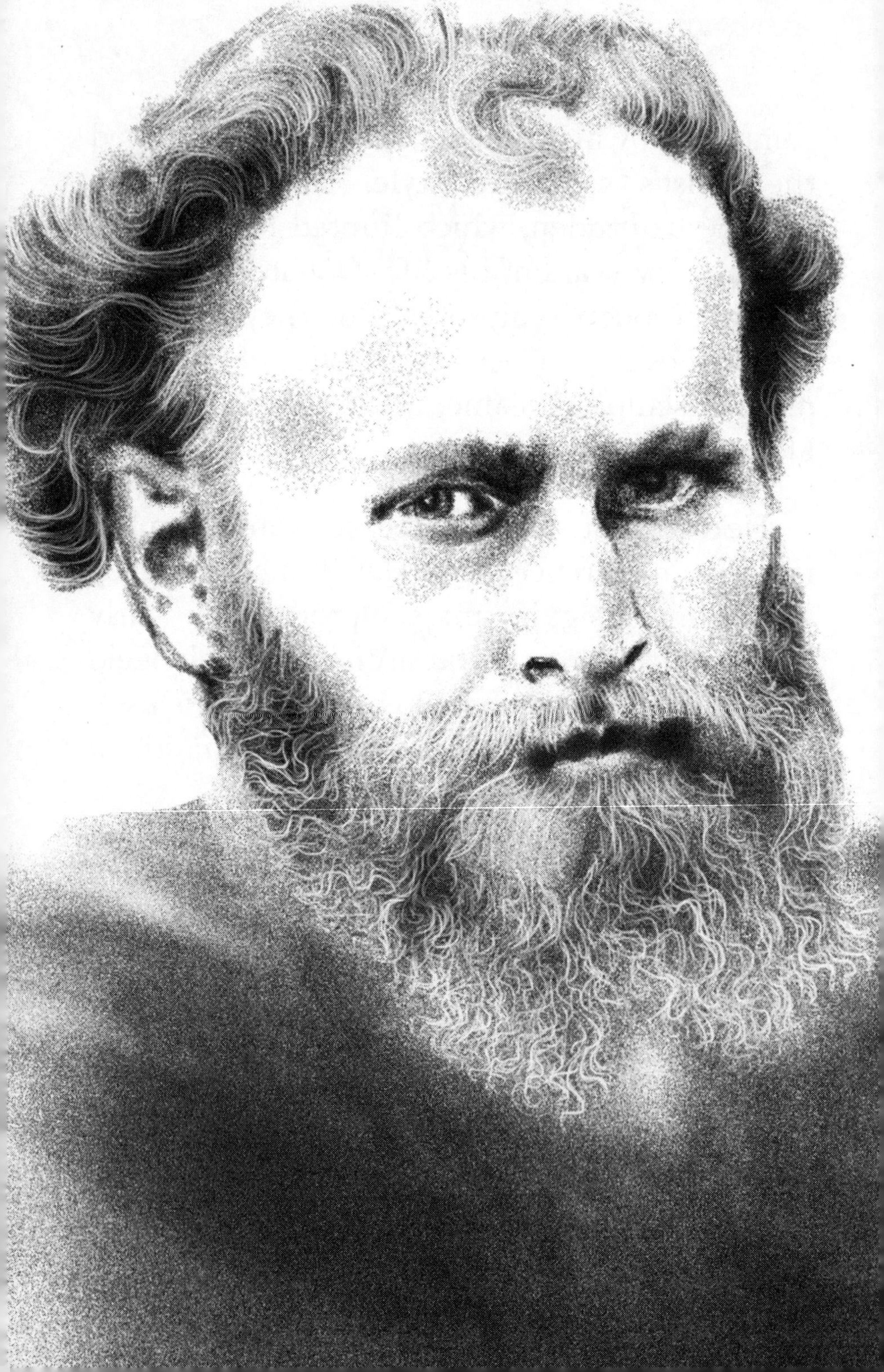

ÉDOUARD MANET

BIRTH: *January 23, 1832*
Paris, France

DEATH: *April 30, 1883 (aged 51)*
Paris, France

Édouard Manet was a French painter. He was one of the major artists who helped transition art from Realism to Impressionism. Manet's major works include *'Olympia'* and *'The Luncheon on the Grass'*.

Édouard Manet was born on January 23, 1832, in Paris, France to Eugénie-Désirée Fournier and Auguste Manet. He was born into a wealthy family in Paris. His father was a high-ranking judge. He wanted his son to become a lawyer, but Manet wanted to join the navy. Upon failing naval examinations, he became an apprentice pilot on a transport vessel. However, he was not the right fit for this kind of job and failed his naval examinations a year later.

Manet learned art from his uncle Edmond Fournier, who encouraged him towards it. Around 1850, Manet attended a painting course where he met Antonin Proust, the future minister of fine arts. Manet traveled to different places like Florence, Rome, Netherlands and Germany. His trips influenced his different styles and art forms. He studied classical works of art and in his free time, he tried to copy the artworks of the masters.

During this time, most of his paintings were rooted in Realism. In 1856, he opened his own studio and made attempts at Realism and creating contemporary art. Manet portrayed everyday-life elements like pavement cafes, bullfights and gypsies in his paintings. He took inspiration from the streets of Paris. He used bold colors and broad brush strokes in all his artworks. He soon discovered his own unique style; Manet didn't like to layer his paints. This painting style influenced the Impressionist artists.

Later in his career, he created artworks based on themes. In 1860, he produced a portrait of his mother and father, and another painting called *'The Spanish Singer'*. These pieces also gained lots of positive reviews from art lovers. His painting *'Music in the Tuileries'* was one of his major works but it remained incomplete.

Throughout his life, Manet used Realism in his art. His aim was to be accepted by the Salon, an official art exhibition in France. For Salon, he submitted *'The Absinthe Drinker'*. The painting depicted an everyday scene of a poor man drinking. But it was rejected. His other major painting was *'The Luncheon on the Grass'*. It was also rejected by the Salon. Manet decided to continue experimentation and explore other art styles.

Manet was criticized for his earlier paintings, as he tried to venture beyond the boundaries of classical paintings. He had a modern painting style and often used photographic lighting. When he became friends with Impressionist artists like Claude Monet and Edgar Degas, he started experimenting with painting outdoors.

Many of the Impressionist artists began their own exhibition separate from the Salon. Napoleon III established the Salon des Refusés to exhibit works rejected by the Salon. But Manet still wanted the approval of the traditional French art critics. In the 1870s, Manet's paintings received significant acclaim. Many of his paintings were finally accepted by the Salon. His art, during that time, influenced the Impressionist style heavily. In the latter part of his career, he created waves with a painting called 'A Bar at the Folies-Bergere'. It was eventually hung in the Salon. Manet was awarded the Legion d'Honneur by the French government. Manet finally received the critical acclaim he so craved near the end of his life.

Manet died on April 30, 1883, at the age of

51 in Paris, France. After his death, many artists kept his legacy going. His lifelong friend Antonin Proust wrote a valuable account of Manet's life as an artist.

Now, he is considered as one of the greatest French artists. He is known as a bridge between Realism and Impressionism. He also paved the way for a new style of art. A few art historians even consider Manet as one of the founding fathers of Modern Art.

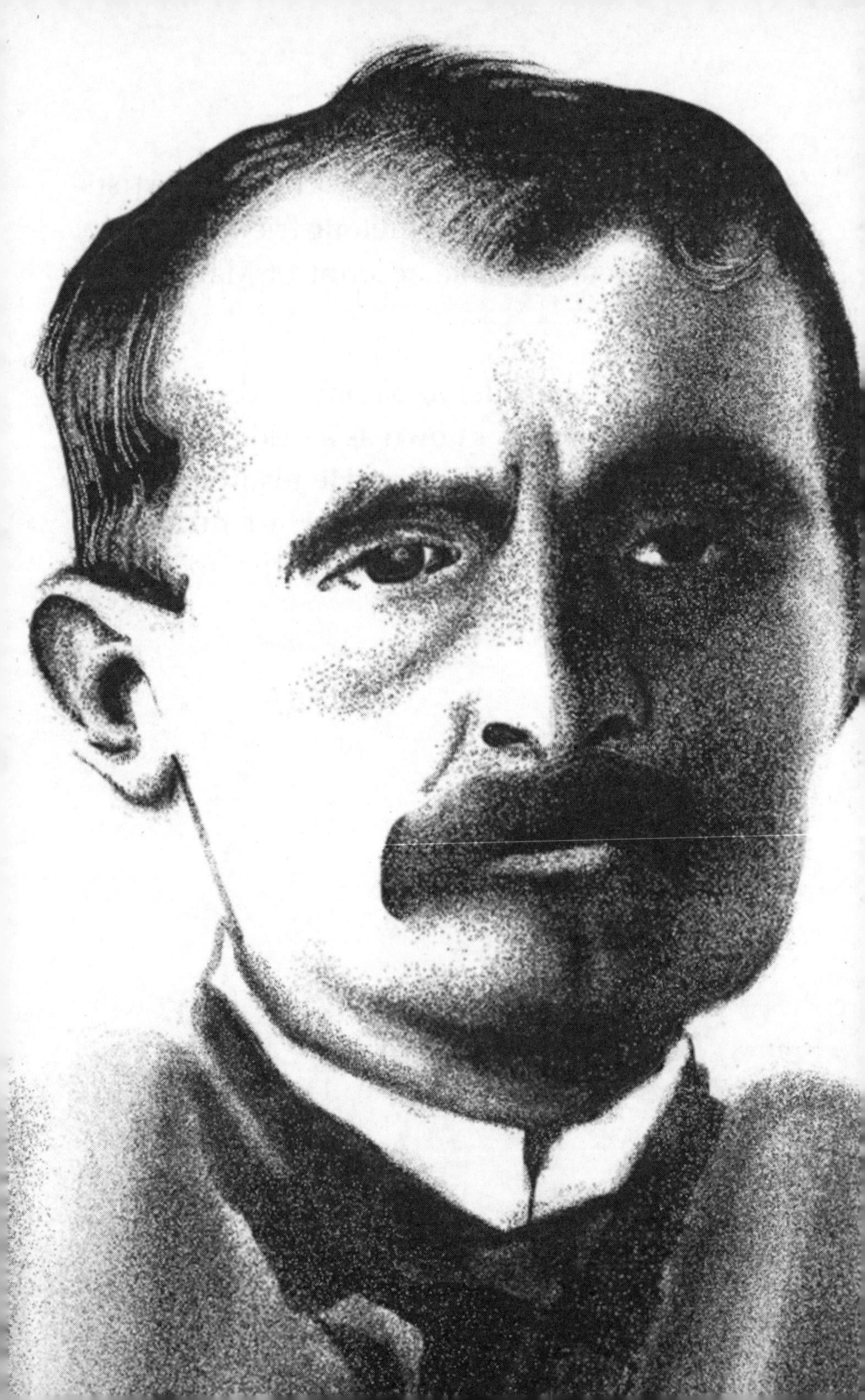

EDVARD MUNCH

❧

BIRTH: *December 12, 1863*
Loten, Norway

DEATH: *January 23, 1944 (aged 80)*
near Oslo, Norway

dvard Munch was a Norwegian painter and printmaker. His most famous painting is *'The Scream'* from 1893. He was a significant part of the Symbolist movement in the 1890s and developed Expressionist art from 1900 onwards.

Edvard Munch was born on 12th December, 1863, in a farmhouse in Norway to Christian Munch and Laura Catherine. His father was a military doctor and a very religious person. When he was just five years old, he lost his mother and soon after, one of his sisters too.

His parents were the ones who introduced him to art. His mother was an artist and his father taught him literature. By the time he was thirteen, he had become a skilled artist. Munch's early paintings were simple, like medicine bottles and other mundane objects. During that time, he met other artists at the Kristiania Bohème, an art association, and was fascinated by their landscapes. Thus, he began to draw oil paintings.

He attended Kristiania Technical College and was trained as an engineer for one year. Even though he excelled in mathematics, physics and chemistry, he realized that painting was his true calling. He decided to quit his ongoing studies and join the Royal School of Art and Design. Munch learned art from the famous sculptor Julius Middelthun, and the painter Christian Krohg. He also rented a studio where he worked with six other artists. Munch's paintings were inspired by Naturalism and Krohg.

He displayed his first painting in 1883 at the Art Exhibition and Autumn Exhibition. For the next few years he traveled abroad. In Paris, he studied different art styles for three weeks. During this period, six of his paintings were exhibited at the Autumn Exhibition. He used a different type of brushstroke technique and color palettes to develop his style. He made another painting called *'Inger on the Beach'* in 1889, portraying his sister. The composition foreshadowed his next collection.

Munch also held his first solo exhibition in the Student Society, in which around sixty paintings were showcased. Following this he received a two-year state scholarship to study in Paris under the French painter Léon Bonnat. That year he lost his father.

In 1890, he spent most of his time with renowned painters and poets of that time. Five of his paintings were lost in a fire including the first version of *'The Day After'*.

In early 1890s, he received the state grant for artists for the third time and traveled to Paris. The National Gallery also bought Munch's first painting, *'Night in Nice'*. In 1892, a famous painter, Adelsteen Normann was impressed by Munch's solo exhibition, which he conducted in Paris. He invited Munch to present his art in Berlin. Munch stayed in Berlin for many years.

He painted almost a random series of paintings called the *'Frieze of Life'* and released them in 1902. Munch released this collection of paintings including the pieces, *'Despair'*, *'Melancholy'*, *'Anxiety'*, and *'Jealousy'*. One of the pieces was his masterpiece called *'The Scream'*. It is one of the most recognizable paintings in the history of art. It represented the anxiety of modern man and was painted with dark colors and simplified forms. It reflected Munch's own mental frame and what would later be the central themes of Existentialism. This collection was a great success and established him as a famous artist.

His paintings were based on the themes of love, pain, anxiety, jealousy and death. He also developed a woodcut and lithographic technique. He also made multi-colored versions of *'The Sick Child'* which became quite famous.

In 1897, Munch earned a good amount of money and bought himself a summer house in Norway. He named it the Happy House and spent every summer there for the next twenty years.

In 1906, Munch studied the art of sculpting and began to produce his own little sculptures. He soon received many orders for portraits and prints. Around 1907, he was more interested in painting human figures and depicting real-life scenarios. Around 1908-09, Munch suffered a mental breakdown that affected his work tremendously. His work lost its melancholy and took a positive turn, without any of its previous intensity.

Munch remained unmarried for life. He spent the latter part of his life in solitude. He died on 23rd January, 1944, at the age of 80 near Oslo, Norway.

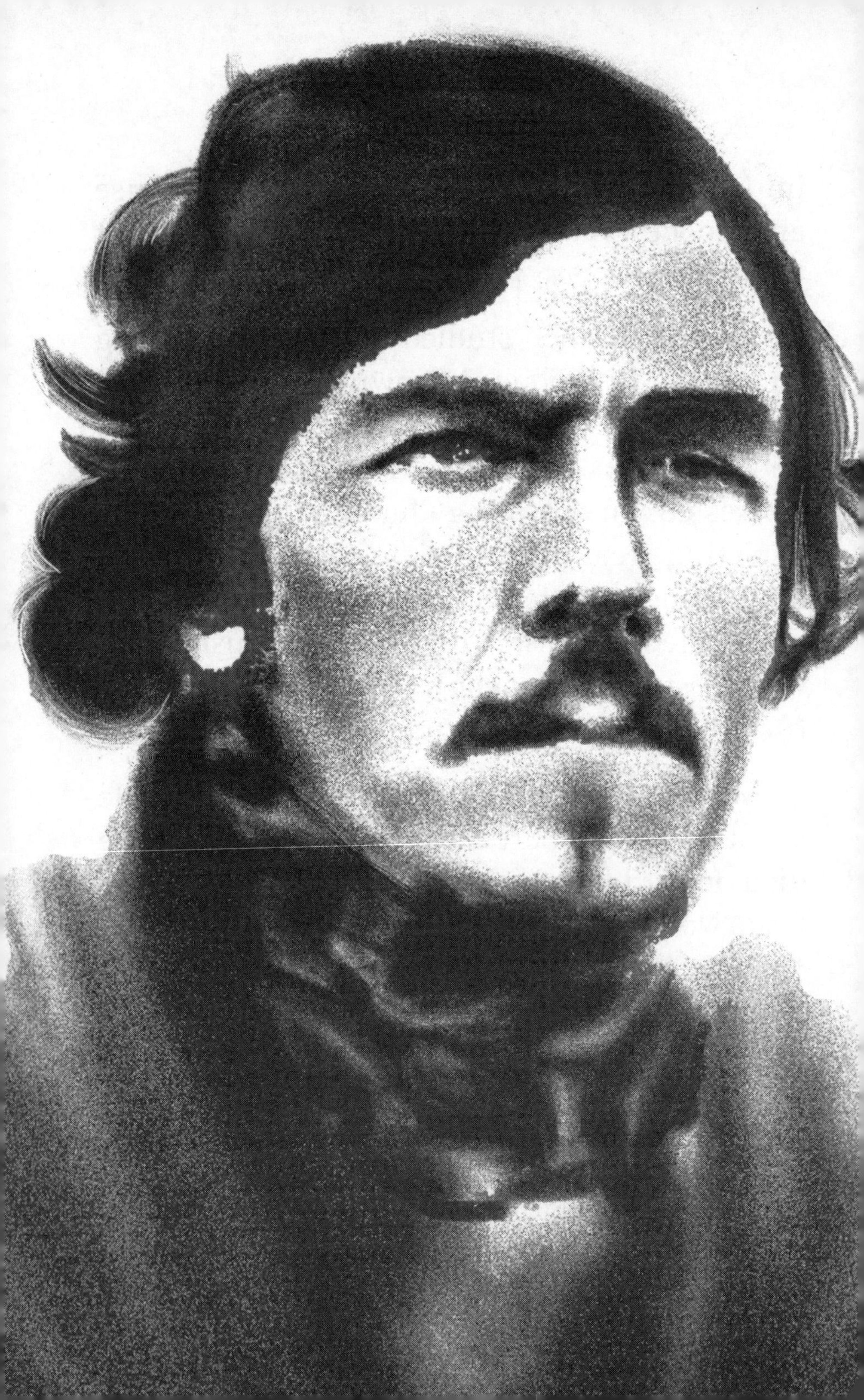

EUGÈNE DELACROIX

BIRTH: *April 26, 1798, France*

DEATH: *August 13, 1863 (aged 65)*
Paris, France

Eugène Delacroix was one of the greatest French Romantic painters, who played an essential part in the development of Impressionist and Post-impressionist paintings through his use of color, inspired by historical and contemporary events and literature.

Eugène Delacroix's full name was Ferdinand-Eugène-Victor Delacroix. He was born on April 26, 1798, in Charenton-Saint-Maurice, France to Charles-Delacroix and Victoire Oeben. His father was a government official who was ambassador to Holland in 1798. He took an interest in art because of his mother, who introduced him to art and literature. By the age of seventeen, he had developed a passion for music and art. He lost his parents at a very young age.

For his education, he attended the Lycee Louis-le-Grand school in Paris, and later he went to the Lycee Pierre Corneille school. He did well academically and won many awards for his paintings. Then, he went to the famous art school in France, Ecole des Beaux-Arts.

His earlier works were inspired by Michelangelo and Peter Paul Rubens. Another painter who influenced Delacroix's art was Theodore Gericault. He was a French pioneer in Romanticist art. Delacroix was naturally influenced by Romanticism given the time period he was born in. He referred to religious and literary subject matters in many of his paintings. Delacroix continued to paint, inspired by the works of Dante, Shakespeare, and the Romantic poet Lord Byron.

Delacroix's first masterpiece was *'Dante and*

Virgil in Hell'. It was inspired by Dante's epic *The Divine Comedy*. It was displayed at the prestigious art exhibition of the Paris Salon. The painting was considered to be a pioneer of the Romantic Movement. Delacroix was commissioned around France for many decorative projects like murals and ceiling paintings, and painting government buildings, which allowed him to practice on a larger scale.

During the 1820s, his painting reflected historical events like the Greek War of Independence and its horrors. His 1824 painting *'The Massacre at Chios'* was inspired by war themes. He beautifully expressed the emotions of different subjects. Pain and misery became common themes in his works. Later, he created *'Greece on the Ruins of Missolonghi'* in 1826. Both works were based on the subjects of history and literature. He used bold colors, and his art style also altered due to his interaction with J.M.W. Turner, Sir Thomas Lawrence and John Constable.

Another one of Delacroix's well-known works was *'The Death of Sardanapalus'*. This painting was based on a tragedy; a somewhat incoherent painting depicting women, slaves, jewels and rich fabrics in a riotous manner. In 1830, his major work was *'Liberty Leading the People'* where he portrayed the French Revolution, more specifically the July Revolution that had brought Louis-Phillipe to the French throne. The overall calm and quiet tone of the painting marked a change in Delacroix's style, which started approaching allegory mixed with contemporary realism. In 1831, the painting was purchased by the Government of France.

The next year, Delacroix traveled to Morocco with King Louis-Philippe. He was so taken by their exuberant culture that he made hundreds of sketches in the duration of his trip. The colors, the horses, the nature and the flowing clothes of the Arabs all inspired his paintings. He became freer with his use of color. Some of his paintings from that time were *'Women of Algiers in Their Apartment'*, *'Jewish Wedding in Morocco'*, *'Arab Saddling His Horse'* and *'Arab Horses Fighting in a Stable'*.

In 1838, he created the painting '*Medea to Kill her Children*'. It was inspired by Greek mythology.

In his later years, Delacroix painted more government buildings. He took the inspiration from Michelangelo. His next works were '*The Battle of Taillebourg*' and '*The Taking of Constantinople*', created in 1840.

Delacroix also developed the forms of Impressionist and Post-impressionist paintings. His style included rough brushstrokes and he experimented with sensuous colors and light. He linked the classic style of the old masters and the modern movements of the 19th century.

Delacroix died on August 13, 1863, in Paris. After his death, thousands of his drawings, watercolors and prints were discovered.

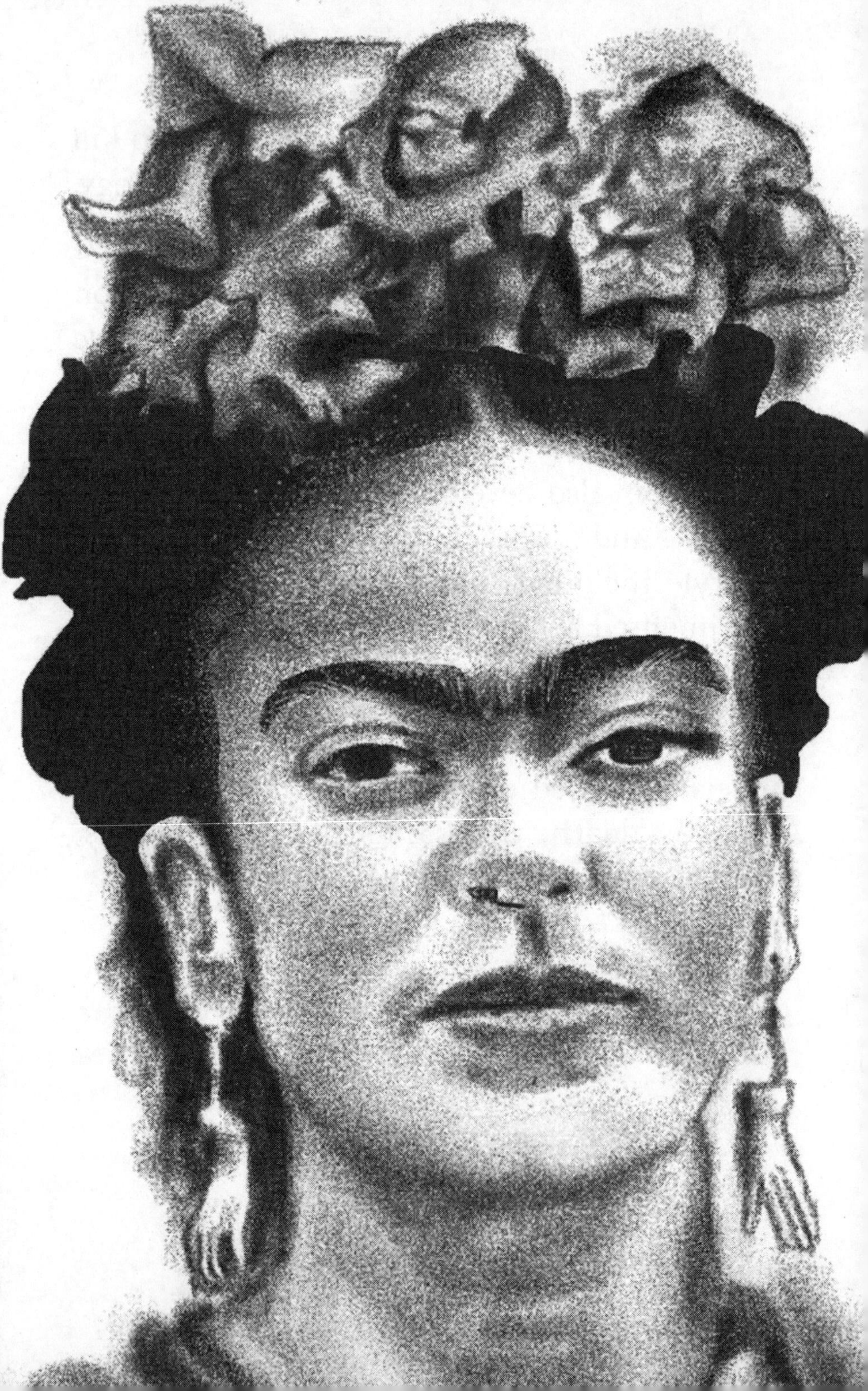

FRIDA KAHLO

BIRTH: July 6, 1907
Coyoacán, Mexico

DEATH: July 13, 1954 (aged 47)
Coyoacán, Mexico

Frida Kahlo was a Mexican painter best known for her extravagantly colored self-portraits and is still hailed as a feminist icon. Her paintings were based on themes such as identity, the human body and death. She was usually identified as a Surrealist. She linked traditional Mexican folk art with Surrealism. Her most famous works include *'Self Portrait with Thorn Necklace and Hummingbird'*, *'Memory, the Heart'*, *'Henry Ford Hospital'*, *'Self Portrait with Monkeys'* and *'What I saw in the Water'*.

Frida Kahlo was born on July 6, 1907, in Coyoacán, Mexico to Guillermo Kahlo, a photographer and Matilde Gonzalez. She had three siblings. Kahlo suffered from poor health in her childhood. At the age of six, she contracted polio and was bedridden for nine months. The polio caused her right leg to grow much thinner than her left one.

After her recovery from polio she had a limp. To fight her disease, she played soccer and learned swimming. She kept a very close relationship with her father her whole life. She learned how to use the camera and develop photographs from him. She attended the famous National Preparatory School in 1922 and worked as an apprentice under Fernando Fernandez. He was a commercial paint-maker and taught Frida the basics of drawing and copy printing.

She was studying medicine until she met with a terrible bus accident in 1925. She was severely injured and had to go through over thirty operations. She stayed in the Red Cross Hospital for several weeks. This accident left her in a great deal of pain. To relieve the pain, she started painting and dabbled in watercolors and oil paintings. She painted more than fifty self-portraits over the course of her life. Kahlo also became politically active and became a member of the Young Communist League.

In 1930, she went to San Francisco and there, she met many prominent artists. The next year, she displayed her works to the public for the first time at the Sixth Annual Exhibition of the San Francisco Society of Women Artists. She presented a portrait of her and Diego Rivera, who she'd met at the National Preparatory School and was infatuated with, called *'Frida and Diego Rivera'*.

In 1937, four of Kahlo's paintings were showcased at the Galeria de Arte, National Autonomous University of Mexico, which was her first public exhibition in Mexico. The following year, she became a good friend of the French poet and Surrealist Andre Breton.

In 1938, she held her first solo exhibition at the Julien Levy Gallery, New York. She displayed

25 of her paintings. Most of her art was sold immediately. The next year, she presented her artwork at the Mexique exhibition in Paris. Her self-portrait named *'The Frame'* was purchased by the largest museum in the world, the Louvre.

Her paintings, *'The Two Fridas'* and *'The Wounded Table'*, were displayed at the International Surrealism Exhibition, held at the Gallery of Mexican Art. Her work led her to meet artists such as Marc Chagall and Pablo Picasso. Her major work from 1940 was *'Self Portrait with Thorn Necklace and Hummingbird'*. In this piece, she painted herself wearing a necklace of thorns, suffering. Her painting was showcased in over 25 museums all over the world.

Kahlo received a commission to paint five important Mexican women from the Mexican government in 1941. But she was unable to finish the project, as she lost her beloved father that year and suffered from many health problems. Despite the challenges, she continued to grow in popularity. In 1942, she painted her *'Self-Portrait with Braid'*.

In 1944, Kahlo painted one of her most famous portraits, *'The Broken Column'*. With this portrait, she put forth the physical challenges she faced. She finished this painting right after she underwent spine surgery.

Her health worsened in 1950 when she was diagnosed with gangrene in her right foot. She became bedridden for months and had several surgeries. But Kahlo continued to work and paint. She created nearly 150 paintings.

For her exceptional work as a painter, she received the National Prize of Arts and Sciences in 1946. In 1929, Frieda married Diego Rivera, a Mexican painter. But they eventually divorced in 1939 before getting back together shortly after in 1940. She died at the age of 47 due to lung failure in Mexico. Kahlo's fame has only grown since her death.

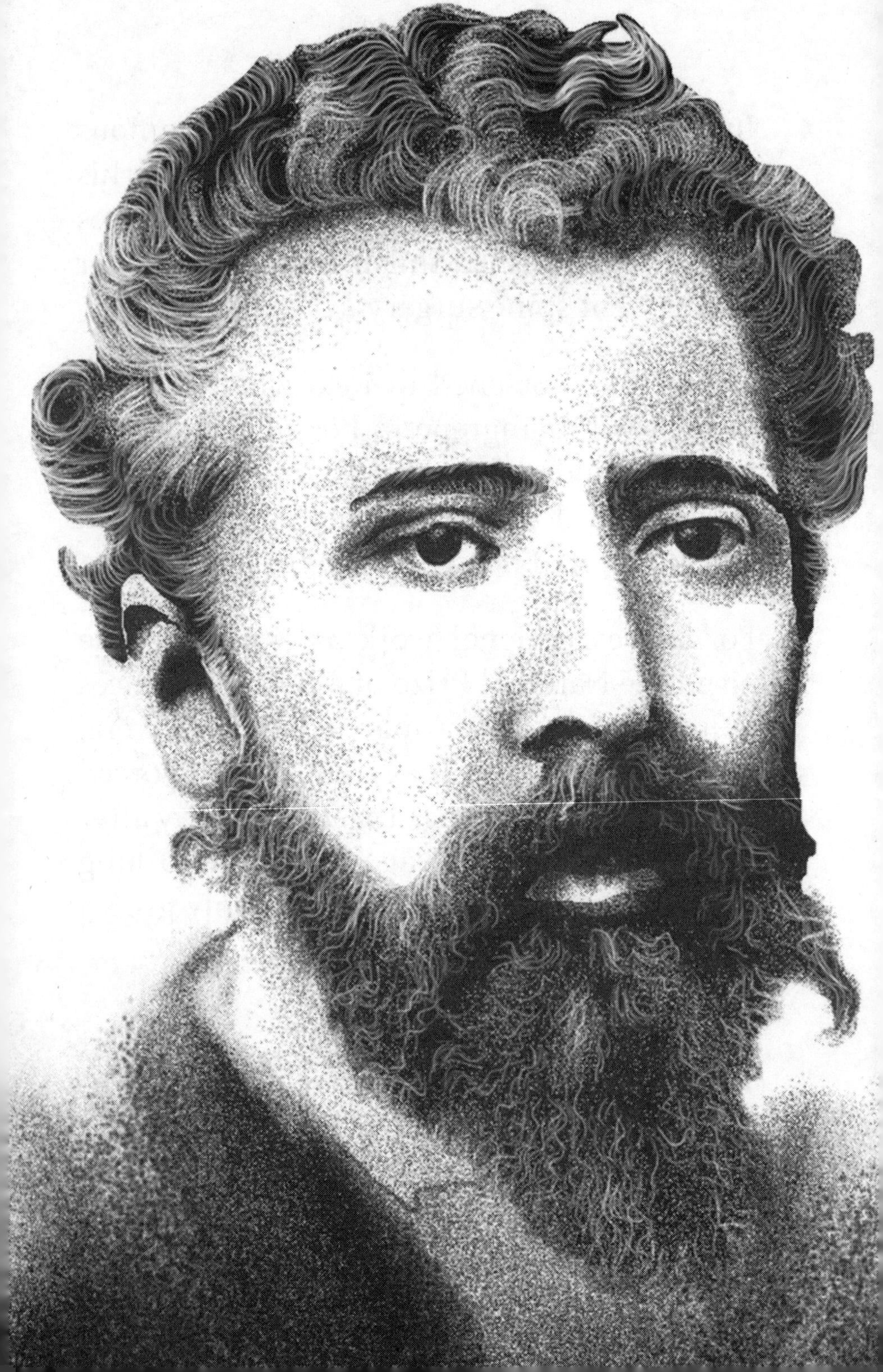

GEORGES SEURAT

BIRTH: *December 2, 1859*
Paris, France

DEATH: *March 29, 1891 (aged 31)*
Paris, France

Georges Seurat was a French painter who founded the famous theory and practice of 19th century Neo-Impressionism. He popularized the technique of using light with tiny brushstrokes, which eventually became "Pointillism". Some of his works include *'Une Baignade'*, *'Asnieres'* and *'A Sunday on La Grande Jatte'*.

Georges Seurat was born on December 2, 1859, in Paris, France. He belonged to a wealthy family, and this allowed him to thrive in his art. His father was a legal official. As a kid, he used to spend his spare time in the garden with his mother. The people who visited him and these places became the subject of many of his greatest paintings. Seurat took an interest in painting from a very early age and studied some great artists' works like the French sculptor Justin Lequien.

For his education, he attended the École des Beaux-Arts in 1878. He excelled in his studies and was an intelligent child who kept to himself. After he served a year in the military, he returned to Paris. Thereon, he began to improve his art skills. For the next two years, he mastered the art of black and white drawings. His parents supported him, which helped Seurat to paint and freely explore different areas of art.

Seurat's greatest work was created in 1883. It was called *'Bathers at Asnieres'*. It was a large painting of people relaxing near the water at Asnieres. He submitted this painting to the official French art exhibition, the Salon. But the Salon rejected his work. Later, he joined the Society of Independent Artists. There, he painted the first of the six large canvases which established his art career.

During this time, Seurat explored different art styles. In the mid-1880s he began to use the science of optics and color in his art. Instead of mixing the paint on the canvas, he experimented by placing tiny dots of different colors next to each other on the canvas. He called this painting style "Divisionism", which was later called "Pointillism". This technique made colors appear brighter. In 1984, he met Paul Signac, who became a good friend and chief disciple of Seurat's. They both used the same method of Pointillism in their art.

In 1884, Seurat created another masterpiece. It was a huge painting called *'Sunday Afternoon on the Island of La Grande Jatte'*. It was also reflected the technique of Pointillism. This iconic piece was painted on a ten-foot wide canvas and displayed as the centerpiece at the last Impressionist exhibition. Many people viewed the work up close and failed to see it whole.

The painting became the most famous image of the 1880s, and he revived the Impressionist movement as it had started to decline. He painted the entire painting with only small dots of bright and pure color. For this piece, he used the same inspiration again, the popular boating place of Asnieres. However, this time, he focused on the island of La Grande Jatte.

Owing to the complexity of the art, it took him two years to finish this project. The painting became the talking point of the exhibition. Most people were amazed by Seurat's art and a few criticized it. But, it made Seurat one of the most significant artists in Paris.

In his later years, he continued to paint in the Pointillism style. He also tried using lines in his art. He believed that different types of lines would express different types of emotions. He also became friends with other Post-impressionist artists such as Vincent van Gogh and Edgar Degas.

Seurat lived with a young model, Madeleine Knobloch for most of his life. In 1890, they had a son. In his last few months, he worked on his final artwork, *'The Circus'*. It was left unfinished, but as if through some premonition, he decided to present it at the eighth Salon des Indépendants. Seurat died very early, on March 29, 1891, at the age of 31 in France. Seurat left a legacy in the art world with his new ideas and concepts for the use of color.

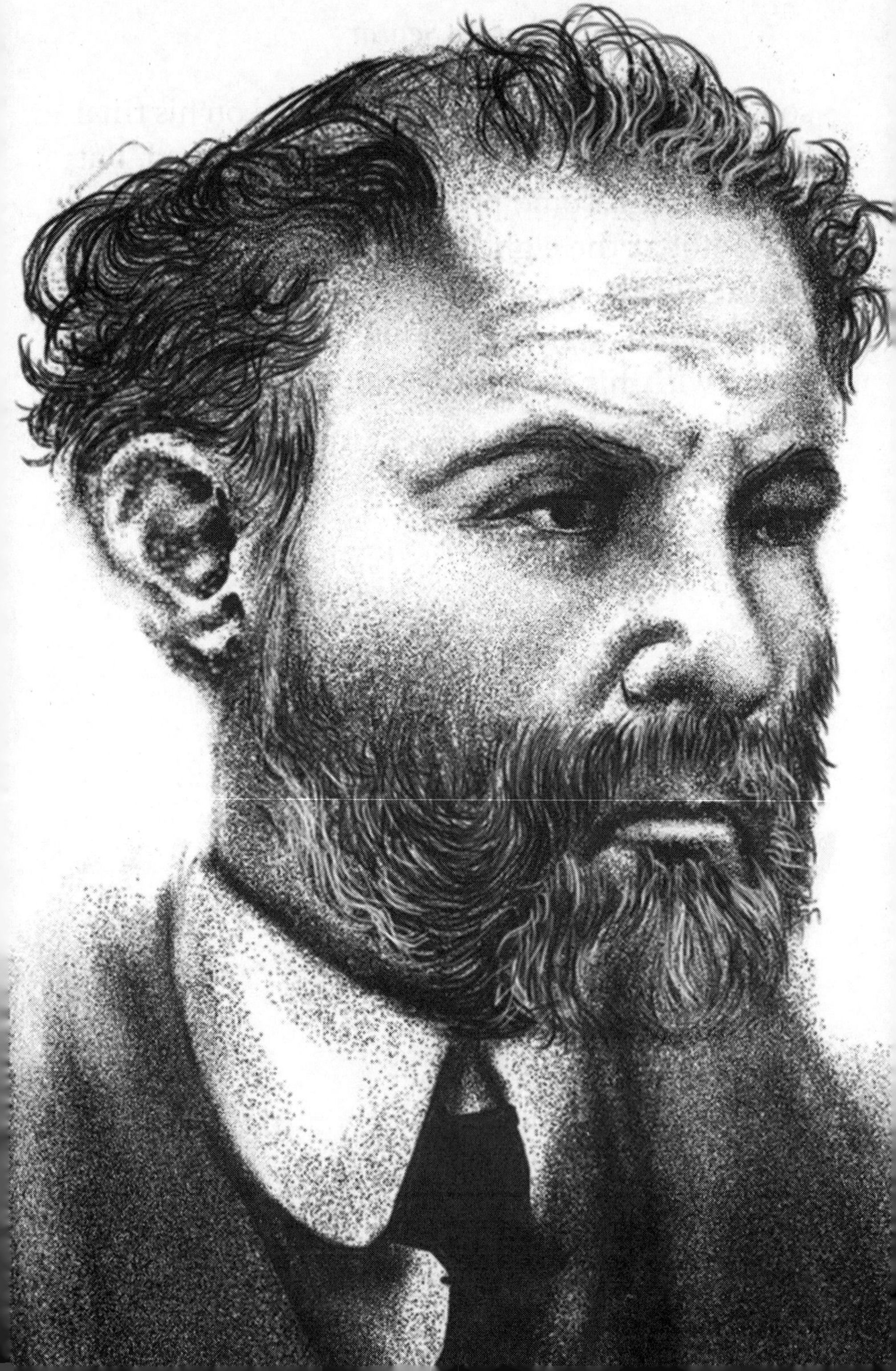

GUSTAV KLIMT

BIRTH: July 14, 1862
Vienna, Austria

DEATH: February 6, 1918 (aged 55)
Vienna, Austria

Gustav Klimt was an Austrian painter and founder of the school of painting called the Vienna Sezession. Klimt dominated the art scene of the 19th century. He was famous for his decorative art, a genre that most of his contemporary artists never adopted. His famous paintings are *'Old Burgtheater in Vienna'*, *'The Kiss'*, *'Portrait of Baroness Elisabeth Bachofen-Echt'* and *'Portrait of Adele Bloch-Bauer I'*.

Gustav Klimt was born in Baumgarten, Austria, to Ernst Klimt and Anne Klimt. He had six siblings. His father worked as a gold and silver engraver in Vienna. His family was poor and Klimt had a difficult childhood. But he somehow completed his education. In 1876, he attended the Vienna School of Arts and Crafts where he studied architectural painting.

Klimt's brother Ernst, who became an engraver, also enrolled in the school. The two brothers and their friend Franz Matsch decided to work together. By 1880, they received many projects working as a team called the Company of Artists. Klimt began to paint wall murals and the ceilings of buildings. His work became popular.

As he continued to develop his style of ornamentation, his mature style emerged, and he founded the Vienna Sezession, a group of painters who revolted against academic art in favor of a highly decorative style similar to Art Nouveau. In 1888, he painted a mural for the Vienna Burgtheater. The painting is recognized for its photographic realism and became popular amongst many artists. During this time, Klimt went through a significant turn of events in his life. He dealt with the loss of his father and brother. All the responsibility fell on his shoulders and he had to provide for his family.

After these events, his artistic skills were never the same again. There was a significant change in his art style. While exploring historical themes, he also ventured into psychology, symbolic themes and started to paint different subjects.

In 1897, he founded the Vienna Sezession and served as president. It was an art society for Austrian artists. Soon, they launched their own magazine called *Sacred Spring.* He was a member of Sezession till 1908. Klimt brought the best foreign artists' works to Vienna and published them in his magazine. He encouraged different art styles like Naturalism, Realism and Symbolism, which all coexisted at the time. The organization even held exhibitions for young artists.

Klimt also developed his own style, which became the movement's trademark. He used Impressionism in his artwork, which was revolutionary against the traditional academic art style. During this time, with the Vienna Sezessionists, he created landscapes like *'Houses on Interact on Attersee Lake'*.

Klimt's work was also controversial. In 1894, he was commissioned to decorate the ceiling of the Great Hall of the University of Vienna. The project took many years to complete, but the three paintings that he created were highly criticized by many people. The three themes on which the art was based were philosophy, medicine and jurisprudence. Because of these liberal themes, his artworks were not appreciated by the public.

Klimt was most successful and appreciated as an artist in his 'Golden Phase', a phase marked by immense success. He started using gold leaf in his painting. Klimt showcased his ornamental style by using a lot of gold and silver colors in his artwork during this time. His major work at this time was *'The Kiss'*, one of the many paintings that were created in his Golden Phase.

His painting, *'Portrait of Adele Bloch-Bauer I'*,

was one of his most prized paintings. For painting *'Death and Life'*, he won many awards and was featured in the World Exhibition in Rome. In 1910, he painted *'Lady with Feather'*.

Throughout his life, Klimt has received honors for his skill and talent in the art field. He was awarded the Golden Order of Merit for his murals in Vienna. He was also an honorary member of the University of Munich and University of Vienna.

Klimt lived with his partner Emilie Louise Floge. They were together for over twenty years. The couple had fourteen children. Klimt died on February 6, 1918, at the age of 55 in Vienna, Austria after he suffered from pneumonia and a stroke.

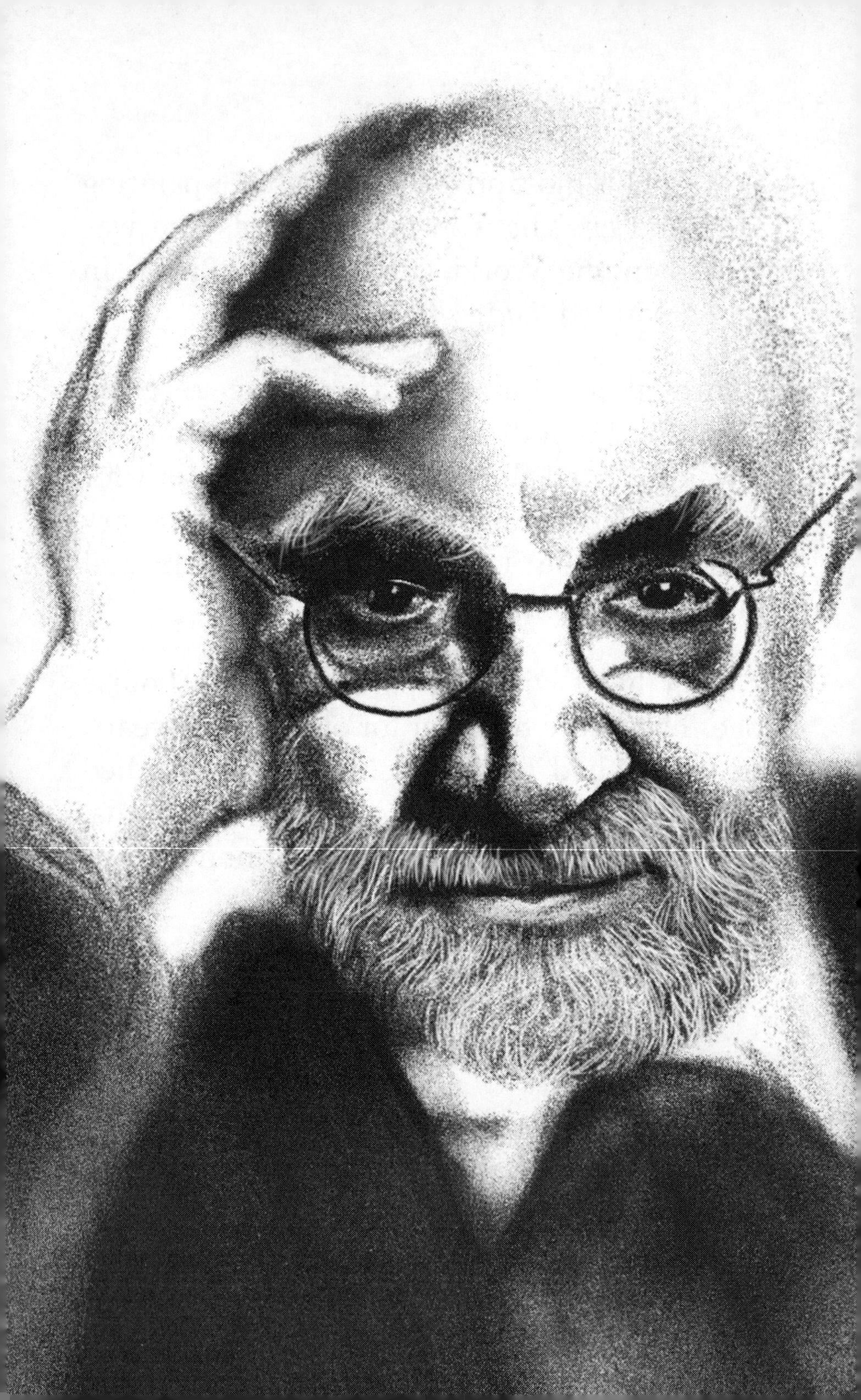

HENRI MATISSE

BIRTH: December 31, 1869
Le Cateau, France

DEATH: November 3, 1954 (aged 84)
Nice, France

Henri Matisse was a French artist whose career spanned over six decades. Apart from being a painter, he was also a draughtsman, printmaker and sculptor. Matisse was one of the major artists of the 20th century. He was a leader of the Fauvist movement.

Henri Matisse's full name was Henri-Émile-Benoît Matisse. He was born on 31st December, 1869 in Nord, France to Émile Hippolyte Matisse and Anna Heloise Gerard.

He was the eldest son of the couple. His father was a grain merchant and a very strict figure in Henri's life. Henri went to Paris to study law at his father's behest in 1887. He started to paint in 1889, when his mother brought him some art supplies when he was recovering from appendicitis. He said it was "a kind of paradise", and made him decide to be an artist, much to his father's chagrin.

After moving to Saint Quentin for some time, he returned to Paris in 1891 and decided to pursue a career in art. He attended an art school called Academie Julian in Paris. When he first began to paint, he took his mother's advice and painted works based on his emotions. He was then trained under the artist Gustave Moreau. With him, Matisse explored modern styles of painting. He learned about contemporary art. Gradually, he started to paint still-life and landscape paintings in a traditional style.

In 1896, he displayed four of his paintings in the Societe Nationale des Beaux-Arts. It was such a success that he was appointed as an associate member of the Salon society. In 1897, Matisse met artist John Peter Russell. He introduced Matisse to impressionism and the famous artist Van Gogh's impressionist art. In the next few years, he advanced to Impressionism. Matisse's first masterpiece was *'The Dinner Table'*, painted in 1897. After getting married in 1898, he moved to London and studied the works of J.M.W. Turner, and also worked in Corsica, where he received a lasting impression of Mediterranean sunlight and color.

Around 1905, he discovered new styles and color techniques. He used bolder, brighter colors and a broad brush stroke. He painted several works for the World Fair at the Grand Palais in Paris.

He started implementing spontaneous brush work and theoretically realistic complementary colors. Matisse and a group of artists displayed their art in a room at the Salon d'Automne. The group was called the "Fauves" meaning "Wild Beasts". Their art style was called Fauvism. Matisse's most famous Fauvist painting was *'Woman with a Hat'*. He used bright and violent colors to paint the woman in this piece. It gained a lot of acclaim and was sought after by major art collectors.

From 1905 to 1906, Matisse painted one of his greatest paintings, *'The Joy of Life'*. It was one of the most important works of 20th century.

In 1911, he completed his *'The Red Studio'*. It was painted towards the end of the Fauvism movement. In this painting, Matisse played with a flatness of the depicted space, almost parallel to the canvas, and created an interesting arrangement of colors and shapes. Later in his life, Matisse changed his art techniques. He used patterns and soon came up with collages. Matisse's cut-outs were huge but showed simplicity. He later produced a book called *Jazz* containing these cut-outs.

During 1906, he traveled to Algeria and Morocco. There, he was inspired by African culture.

By 1919, Matisse had become an internationally known master. His style at that time was characterized by the use of pure colors and their complex interplay. The goal of Matisse's art was the portrayal of joyful living in contrast to the stresses of our technological age.

Other artwork created by Matisse includes paintings such as *'The Blue Nude'*, *'The Knife Thrower'*, and *'Icarus'*. His painting *'The Dance II'*, painted in 1932, highlighted features like simplicity, color and paper cut-outs

One of Matisse's final works was *'Blue Nude II'*, a series of paintings created in 1952. The color blue dominated the painting.

Matisse married Amelie Noellie Parayre in 1898. They got divorced in 1939. He was the father of three children. He died on November 3, 1954, at the age of 84 in Nice, France after he suffered from a heart attack.

Matisse is recognized as one of the founders of Fauvism and one of the leading figures of modern art.

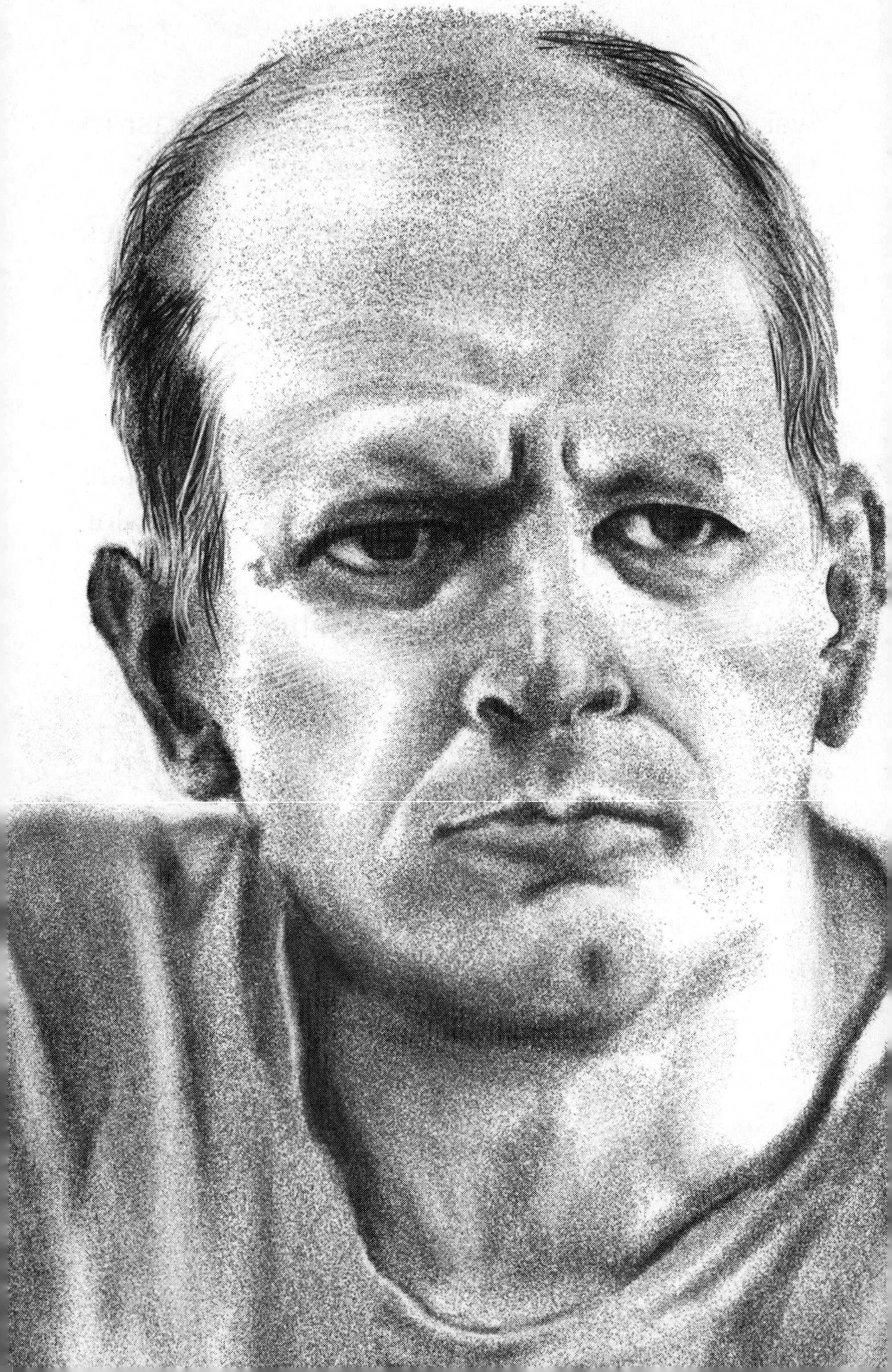

JACKSON POLLOCK

BIRTH: January 28, 1912
Cody, Wyoming, USA

DEATH: August 11, 1956 (aged 44)
East Hampton, New York, USA

Jackson Pollock was an American artist. He was a leading exponent of the Abstract Expressionism movement which is characterized by "action painting". He was one of the pioneers of modern art. Most of his works were influenced by the American painter Thomas Hart Benton.

Paul Jackson Pollock was born on January 28, 1912, in Wyoming to LeRoy Pollock and Stella May McClure. He had four elder brothers. His father worked as a land surveyor for the government. In 1928, they moved to Los Angeles, where Pollock enrolled at Manual Arts High School. Soon, he got interested in art and decided to make a career in it. Later, he traveled all around America and got familiar with American culture. These experiences heavily influenced his later works.

During 1930, he shifted to New York City with his eldest brother, Charles. Both of them attended the Art Students League. There, he was trained by famous American painter Thomas Hart Benton. His teacher taught him different art styles, which made a significant impact on his art career. He worked for the mural division of the WPA Federal Art Project and the Federal Arts Project (FAP). This gave him financial stability during the rest of the Great Depression, and also allowed him to develop his art.

Pollock experimented with the liquid painting technique for his artwork. He developed a new art form which was known as the drip painting technique. He was quite known for not using traditional paint brushes to create images. Instead, he used sticks, hardened brushes and syringes as painting tools. This dripping technique inspired what was later known as "action painting". These paintings were extremely personal as Pollock immersed himself in them as he worked.

Pollock used his entire body to paint. He would place his canvases on the floor to paint on them and never mounted them on a wall. He would apply paint from all directions, which gave his paintings a multi-directional perspective.

This method became popular in America during the 1950's. The technique made him one of the most influential painters at the time, even though he was also highly criticized for his drip paintings. His painting *'One: Number 31'* is amongst the most popular modern paintings.

Pollock was a big name in the art industry during this time. He received lots of commissioned work. For his other paintings, he created dark artwork in which he used deeper shades. Pollock made a collection of black paintings, which were painted on canvases. Later on, he went back to colorful and abstract paintings. He created paintings like *'Autumn Rhythm'* in 1950. He primarily used the colors black and white.

His art was interpreted differently by everyone. That's why most of his paintings didn't have names. Instead, he numbered them. A few of his other paintings were *'Scent'* and *'Search'*. His painting *'Blue Poles'* was also a well-known masterpiece.

Pollock married painter Lee Krasner in 1945. He died on August 11, 1956, at the age of 44 in New York in a fatal car accident. After his death, his wife took care of his possessions. The Pollock-Krasner Foundation was founded by Krasner to help out young, promising artists. An exhibition was held in December 1956 at the Museum of Modern Art, New York in his memory. As a famous modern artist, his artistry and creativity still inspire people even after his death.

In 1989, Jackson Pollock's biography: *Jackson Pollock: An American Saga* was written by Steven Naifeh and Gregory White Smith.

Jackson Pollock

Pollock revolutionized American art history. He was the first abstract artist who was taken seriously by the European artists and was the first American artist to receive so much recognition on a national platform for his work.

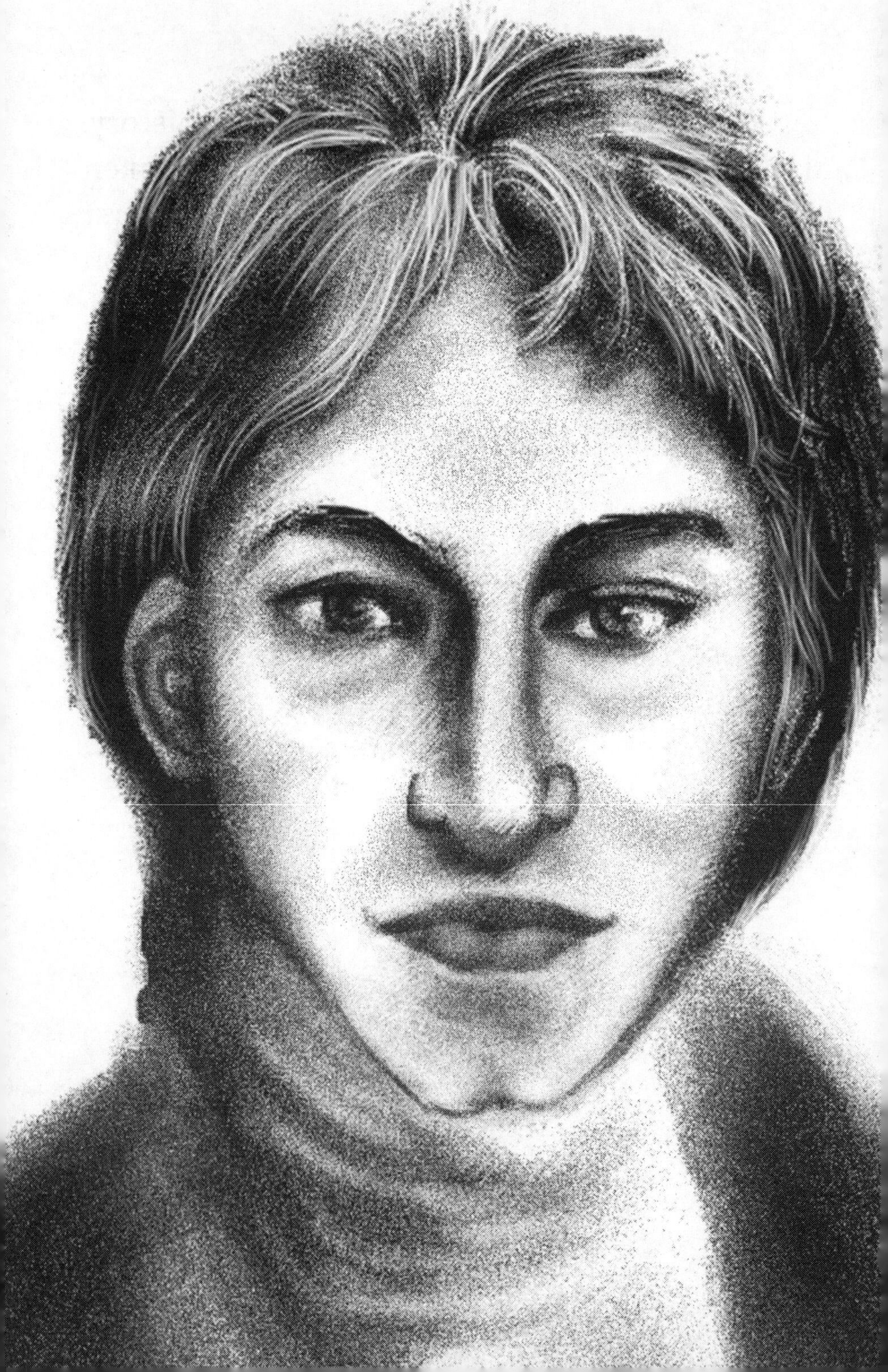

J.M.W. TURNER

BIRTH: April 23, 1775
London, England

DEATH: December 19, 1851 (aged 76)
London, England

Joseph Mallord William Turner was an English Romantic landscape painter. He was best-known for the study of light, color and atmosphere in his paintings. Some of his famous paintings include *'Fishermen at Sea'*, *'Rain'* and *'Steam and Speed'*. He is still recognized as an influential painter of the 19th century and a beacon of the Impressionist movement.

Joseph Mallord William Turner was born on April 23, 1775, in London, England, to William Turner and Mary Marshall. His father was a barber.

When he was around twelve, he sold his first painting to one of his father's customers. His father was amazed by his son's creativity. So, he decided to send him to art school. At the age of fourteen, Turner attended the Royal Academy. He studied other artists' works which influenced his art later on. In 1793, the Royal Academy awarded him for his work. From 1792 onwards, he spent his summers touring the country in search of subjects, filling his sketchbooks with drawings to be worked up later into finished watercolors.

He learned to paint antique structures and also drew the human body. He became skilled at using watercolors. Many of his artworks were published in magazines.

Around 1796, he began to display his oil and watercolor paintings at the Royal Academy. Turner created his first oil painting in 1796. It was called *'Fishermen at Sea'*. The art was famous for its moonlit view. It received positive reviews from art critics. His artwork was compared with that of other famous painters.

Turner traveled in search of inspiration. He visited Wales, Yorkshire and the Lake District, the Midlands, Scotland, and the European continent in between 1792 to 1801.

In 1799, at the youngest permitted age (which was 24), Turner was elected an associate of the Royal Academy, and in 1802 he became a full academician. In 1807, Turner became a professor of perspective at the Royal Academy, where he lectured till 1828.

He used to make copies of the rough drawings of John Robert Cozens, a landscape painter. This influenced Turner to try out landscape painting. He eventually became the greatest landscapist of the 19th century.

Turner's middle years brought a change in his style. His work became bright and atmospheric. The major focus in his art during this time was on the effects of light. His paintings such as

'*St. Mawes at the Pilchard Season*' and '*Frosty Morning*' all focused on atmospheric quality.

He also continued to travel around the globe. He spent a few months in Rome, Florence and Venice. He created thousands of drawings, which he eventually turned into paintings. He used purer and brighter colors. Other works of Turner such as '*The Bay of Baiae with Apollo and Sibyl*' were part of Turner's progress as an artist. He treated oil paints as watercolors and made the colors almost transparent.

The last few years of his life were spent abroad. He visited Italy, Switzerland, Germany and France. He created artworks based on architecture such as '*The Fighting Temeraire*' in 1838. It was a tribute to the passing age of ships, which were replaced by steam-powered vessels.

He also discovered a new, more fluid style that suggested movement and space. During this time, his art was influenced by Impressionism.

He paid less attention to details and more to

natural phenomenon like the sea, the storm, the fire and the sun. His masterpieces followed the themes of rain, steam and speed; he emphasized hue and light. Most of Turner's works were related to the Impressionist style of painting. Turner's artwork later influenced brilliant artists like Monet, Degas, and Renoir.

As years passed, Turner's paintings showed the dissolution of forms. The objects in the paintings became less recognizable. One of the examples of this type of painting was *'The Sunrise with Sea Monsters'*. The sea monsters therein could barely be made out.

Turner remained unmarried all his life, however he was allegedly the father of two daughters. He died on December 19, 1851, in London, England at the age of 76.

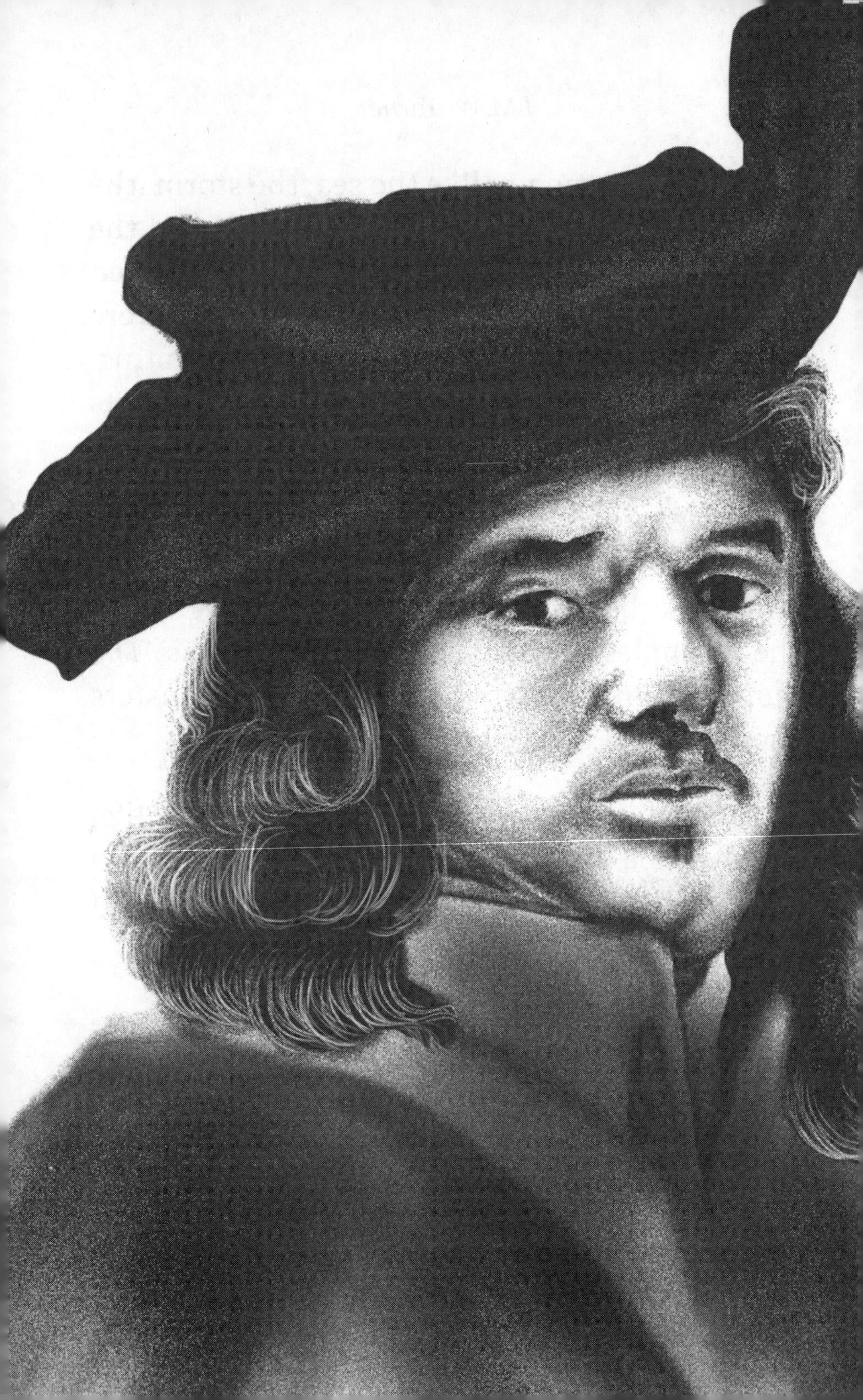

JOHANNES VERMEER

BAPTISEMENT: *October 31, 1632*
Delft, Netherlands

DEATH: *December 15, 1675*
Delft, Netherlands

Johannes Vermeer was a Dutch artist and an art legend. Only around 36 masterpieces of his have survived through time, and these are treasured in the world's most famous museums. His style was highly influenced by everyday scenes and other Golden Age artists. Vermeer's most famous work was the *'Girl with a Pearl Earring'*.

Johannes Vermeer was born on 31st October,

1632 in the Netherlands to Reynier Jansz and Digna Baltens. He had one older sibling. From his early days, he was also known as "Jan". His father was a weaver and an art dealer.

Vermeer inherited both an inn and the art-dealing business upon his father's death in October 1652. In 1641, Janszoon bought a larger inn and named it the Mechelen. There, he sold paintings and became an art dealer.

Consequently, Vermeer developed an interest in painting and decided to pursue a career in art. It was believed that Vermeer's art style was similar to the painter Caravaggio's and that he was the one who taught Vermeer about art. But many believe that Vermeer taught himself to paint. In 1653, Vermeer was selected as a member of a union of painters called the Guild of Saint Luke. It was a business association for painters. In 1662, Vermeer was elected as the head of the guild. During that time, he was viewed as a talented craftsman by other artists.

Around 1657, he created some of his most famous works. At the age of 24, he painted

'*The Procuress*', in which he experimented with oil paints. The same year he met a local art collector Pieter van Ruijven, who supported him financially as a patron. He was amongst the great artists of the Golden Age. His peers were Pieter de Hooch, Gabriel Metsu, Nicolaes Maes and others.

Around the same time he produced two of his major works. The first one was '*The Little Street*', which was an oil painting. And the second one was '*The Milkmaid*', in which he explored a theme common in his paintings: domestic life. In 1659, he painted '*The Girl with the Wine Glass*' and '*View of Delft*'. After that, he worked slowly but at a consistent pace. He took his time to create his masterpieces and produced three paintings in a year. In 1665, he completed the '*Music Lesson*'.

The most famous work of this Dutch artist was '*The Girl with a Pearl Earring*'. It was an oil painting on canvas and inspired many artists. The portrait was done in the Baroque style. The next few works of Vermeer included the

'Art of Painting', *'The Astronomer'* and *'The Geographer'*. His *'Art of Painting'* was regarded as one of the most complex works produced by him.

In the year 1672, he continued to paint and create *'The Allegory of Faith'*, *'The Love Letter'*, and *'Lady Seated at a Virginal'*. That year was known as the 'Year of Disaster', in which many economic crises struck Netherlands. Amidst all of this, the art market collapsed. It harmed Vermeer's business as an art dealer. Vermeer faced dire poverty and his art career suffered a great loss.

Vermeer's paintings were mainly based on the domestic interior scenes. He created large pieces, portraits and also a few cityscapes. He used to get his inspiration from the seventeenth century Dutch society. He also explored religious and scientific themes in his artworks. He mostly used the *'Pointille'* technique in his work. It involved the application of transparent colors to the canvas very loosely. He used natural ultramarine, a brilliant deep-blue color in his paintings. Even though he faced poverty in the year of disaster, Vermeer continued to use natural ultramarine (quite an extravagant substance, rarely used by a new artist) in his art, like in the *'Lady Seated at a Virginal'*.

Vermeer was married to Catherina Bolenes. Vermeer and his wife were happily married for 22 years. He was the father of eleven children.

Vermeer sold most of his art to the wealthiest citizens of Delft, on the advice of his mother-in-law, Maria. But, he never left his hometown and solely relied on local support for his commissions. He never marketed his works and talent elsewhere.

Vermeer died in December 1675. After his death, his wife saved as many of his paintings as possible. She sold most of his artworks to clear her husband's debt.

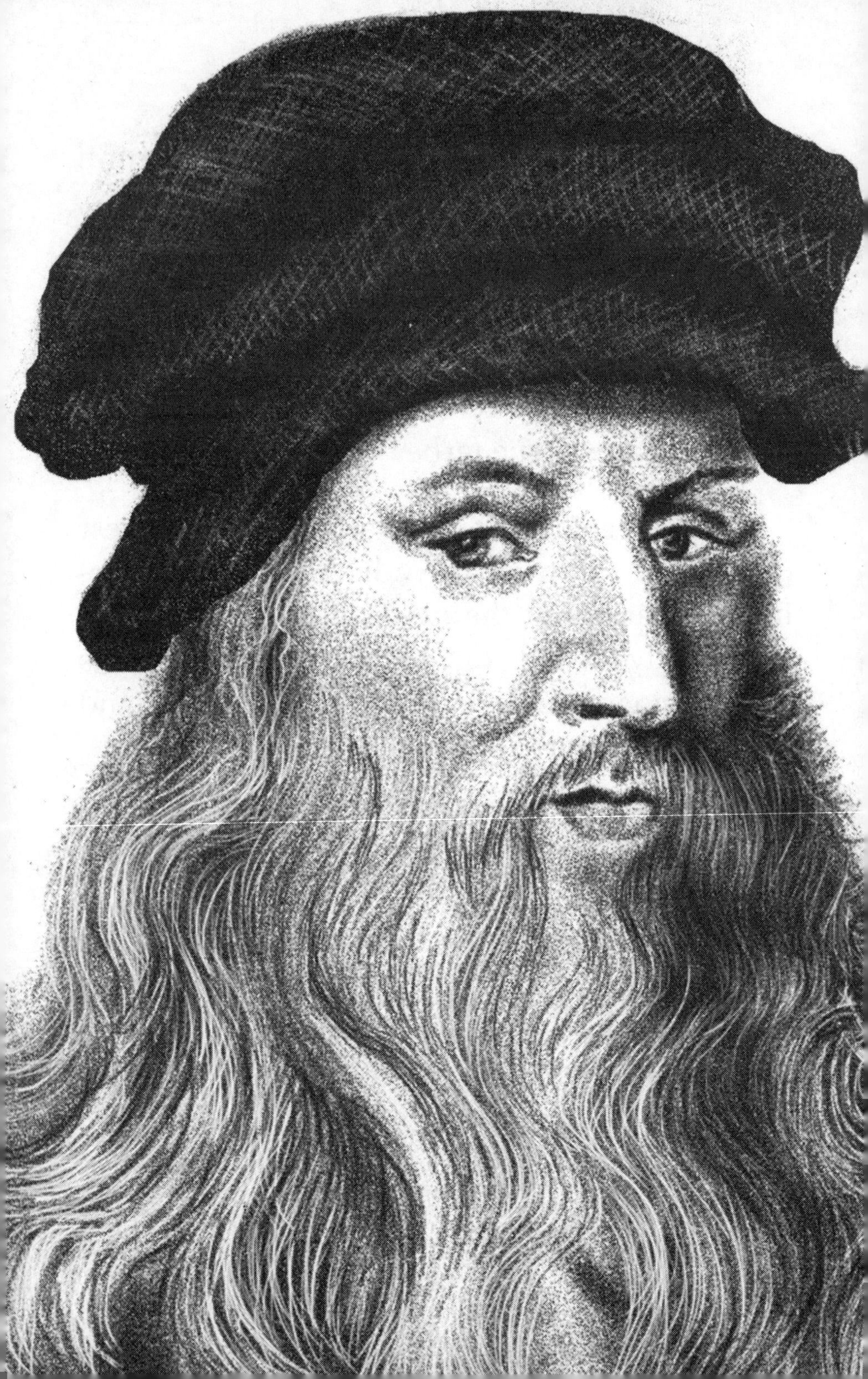

LEONARDO DA VINCI

❧

BIRTH: April 15, 1452
Vinci, Italy

DEATH: May 2, 1519 (aged 67)
France

Leonardo da Vinci was a famous artist, sculptor, architect and engineer of the Italian Renaissance. He was best known for his works such as *'The Last Supper'* and the *'Mona Lisa'*, arguably some of the most famous paintings in the world. He was also a great inventor and theorized many scientific concepts. He developed new art methods that are still used to this day.

Leonardo da Vinci's full name was Leonardo

di Ser Piero da Vinci. He was born on April 15, 1452, in Vinci, Italy to Ser Pierro da Vinci and Caterina. It was believed that he spent a few years of his life in Antonio. Later, he lived with one of his uncles in the town of Vinci. Da Vinci received no formal education beyond basic reading, writing and math in his early years, but his father appreciated his artistic talent.

From a very young age, Leonardo showed incredible artistic ability. When he was fourteen, he became an apprentice under the famous artist Andrea del Verrocchio. Verrocchio taught him drawing, painting and more. He remained his apprentice until 1477.

Leonardo finally chose art as his primary career. He used all that he had learned at the workshop in his artwork. He worked with Verrocchio on a few of his paintings, one of them being *'The Baptism of Christ'*. One of his earliest pieces was *'Arno Valley'* in 1473, which he also made with the help of his teacher. It was a sketch of the Arno Valley made with ink on paper.

His mentor truly believed Leonardo was far too superior as an artist.

Somewhere between 1478 and 1480, he painted *'Madonna of the Carnation'*. It was an oil painting depicting Mother Mary with baby Jesus on her lap. His other masterpieces were *'The Virgin of The Rocks'* and *'Madonna of the Rocks'*. Contrary to popular rumors these are two different paintings, created for the same commissioning. However, the verdict is still out on how much of a role Da Vinci played in the creation of the second piece, which now hangs in the National Gallery, London. He even created a huge horse out of clay named the *'Gran Cavallo'*, commissioned in 1482 to be the most monumental equestrian statue in the world but it remained unfinished.

One of his most famous paintings, *'The Last Supper'*, was created in 1498. The painting remains one of his most highly reproduced works of art.

Later, Leonardo went to Florence and began

painting *'The Battle of Anghiari'*. He worked on it for three years, and yet it remained unfinished. At the same time, he started painting his ultimate masterpiece, the *'Mona Lisa'*.

Today, the painting is regarded as a national treasure. Mona Lisa's smile has been interpreted in many different ways. It has been the subject of many research studies, experiments and debates.

Leonardo did little painting while in France, spending most of his time arranging and editing his scientific studies, his treatises on painting and anatomy. He also came up with designs that resemble various modern inventions.

Leonardo maintained diaries which contained thousands of pages of notes and drawings on natural philosophy, life and travel. He wrote about his scientific knowledge and inventions. These diaries contained everything about Da Vinci's life. His inventions were much ahead of his time. His work in science and engineering was as impressive as his art. He planned other projects such as the construction of a canal for sustainable water supply in the city.

'*The Vitruvian Man*' was created by him around 1487; it was accompanied by his notes based on the notes of the architect, Vitruvius Pollio. It was an attempt to relate man to nature. He even wrote books throughout his lifetime; one being the *Codex on the Flight of Birds*. It was a scientific document which contained eighteen folios.

He remained unmarried all his life. He died at the King's manor house on May 2, 1519, at the age of 67.

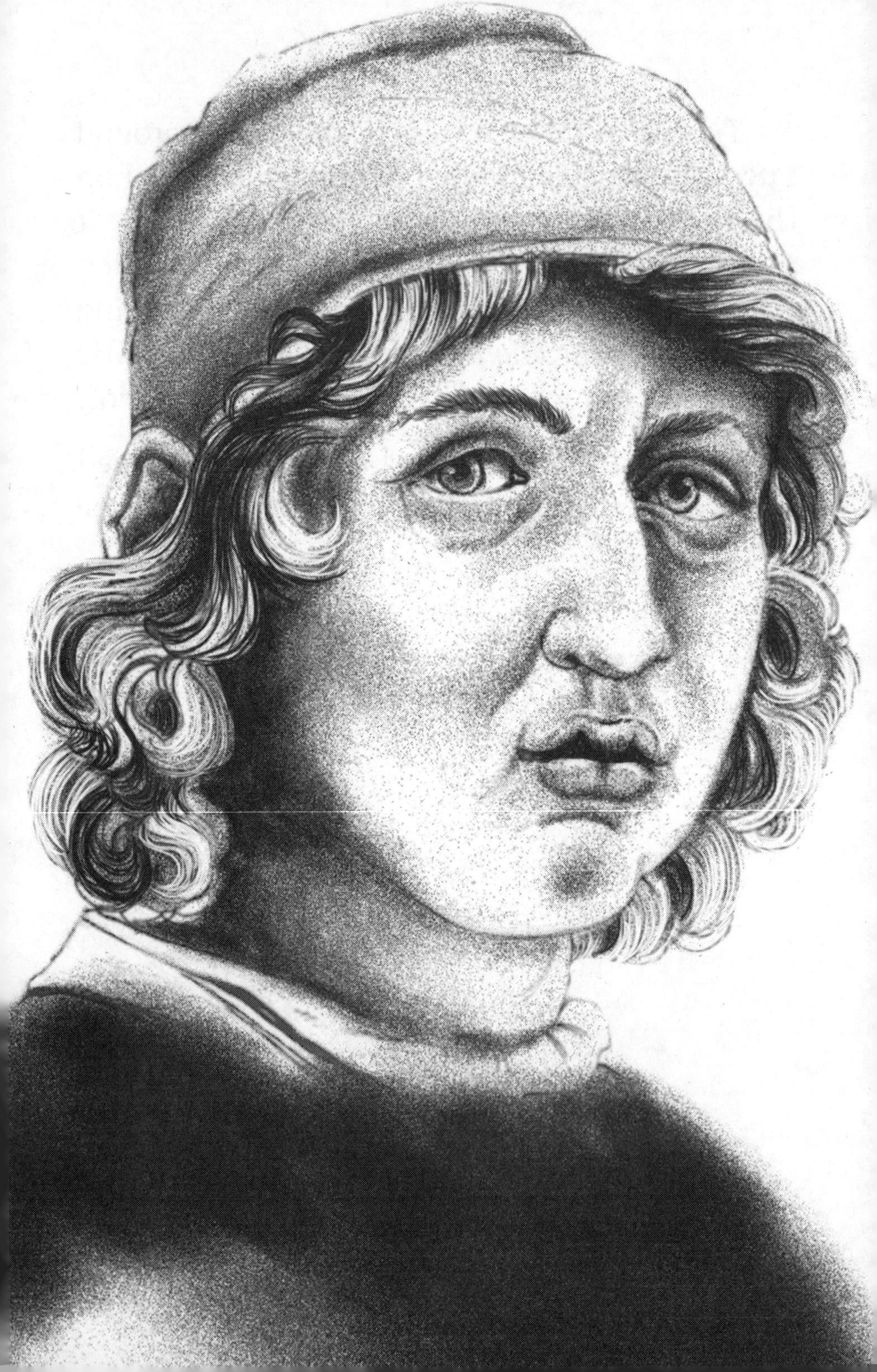

MASACCIO

BIRTH: *December 21, 1401*
San Giovanni Valdarno, Italy

DEATH: *1428*
Rome, Italy

asaccio was an Italian painter. He was one of the most notable painters of the early Renaissance era. Sometimes, he is referred to as the "Father of the Renaissance". He introduced art styles like the *'Vanishing Point'* and *'Linear Perspective'* and brought a three-dimensional effect in some of his paintings. Masaccio's famous works include the *'Holy Trinity'*, *'San Giovenale Triptych'* and *'The Expulsion from the Garden of Eden'*.

Tommaso di Giovanni di Simone Cassai's

life is mostly undocumented and very few records are available. It is believed that he was born on December 21, 1401 in Italy to Ser Giovanni di Mone Cassai and Monna Lacoula. He had one sibling. His father worked as an official in the government. But the family was traditionally engaged in carpentry. Throughout his life, Masaccio solely cared about painting and was often called "clumsy" or "whimsical". He never bothered about people, politics and the government.

Most of the novice painters, at the time, sought training under the guidance of an established artist. Masaccio certainly must have apprenticed as well, however no record of that remains. This has made it difficult to pin down his influences since a lot of Renaissance art was born from imitation.

In the late 1420's, Masaccio became a member of Florentine Arte dei Medici e Speziali, a painters' society in Florence.

Masaccio's first painting was called the *San Giovenale Triptych* made in 1422. He dominated most of the Renaissance era. This painting showed the sort of influence that the Florentine school of painting had had on Masaccio as a young artist. He was influenced by the works of Donatello and Brunelleschi. Together, the three founded the Renaissance.

During 1424, he completed *'Madonna and Child with Saint Anne'*. Masaccio was famous for his three-dimensional paintings and also for the Realism that he showed in his portraits. He used a single light source and gave dimension to the human body in his art. For this painting, he collaborated with artist Masolino da Panicale. He also worked with Panicale for the rest of his career.

In 1425, Masaccio produced his most famous work called *'The Expulsion from the Garden of Eden'*. This represented the banishment of Adam and Eve from the Garden of Eden. The highlight of the piece was the expressions on the faces of the figures. Masaccio completed another famous painting *'The Tribute Money'* the same year. It rivals Michelangelo's David as an icon of Renaissance art.

Masaccio was offered a project to paint an altarpiece for the Church of Santa Maria del Carmine, located in Pisa in 1426. It was one of the most important works of his career. One of the Church's paintings was called *'Madonna and the Child'*. It was considered as his most important work, from an artistic perspective.

In the year 1427, the painter started his most popular work called the *'The Trinity'*. It was created for the Church of Santa Maria Novella. The Trinity depicted the Father, the Son and the Holy Spirit shown as one. It was regarded as the greatest masterpiece of his career.

Masaccio noticed that illustrated artworks that showed biblical stories or figures had become popular, so he started employing the same art style. He painted a collection of biblical paintings, which narrated the stories through paints. Masaccio was highly sought after by various churches across Italy and created captivating artwork. During the Renaissance period, art was often passed down from father to son. But, Masaccio and his brother's artistry were linked to their grandfather, who was a carpenter.

There was no record of Masaccio getting married in his lifetime. He died in 1428 at the age of 26. Even though he was not as popular as other Renaissance-era artists, he still thrived in his own way. The light atmosphere showcased in Masaccio's artwork, significantly matched the artist Giotto's style.

Masaccio used a more realistic approach towards his art. It was stated that prominent artists such as Leonardo da Vinci, Michelangelo, and Raphael, were amazed by the sculptural techniques in Masaccio's work.

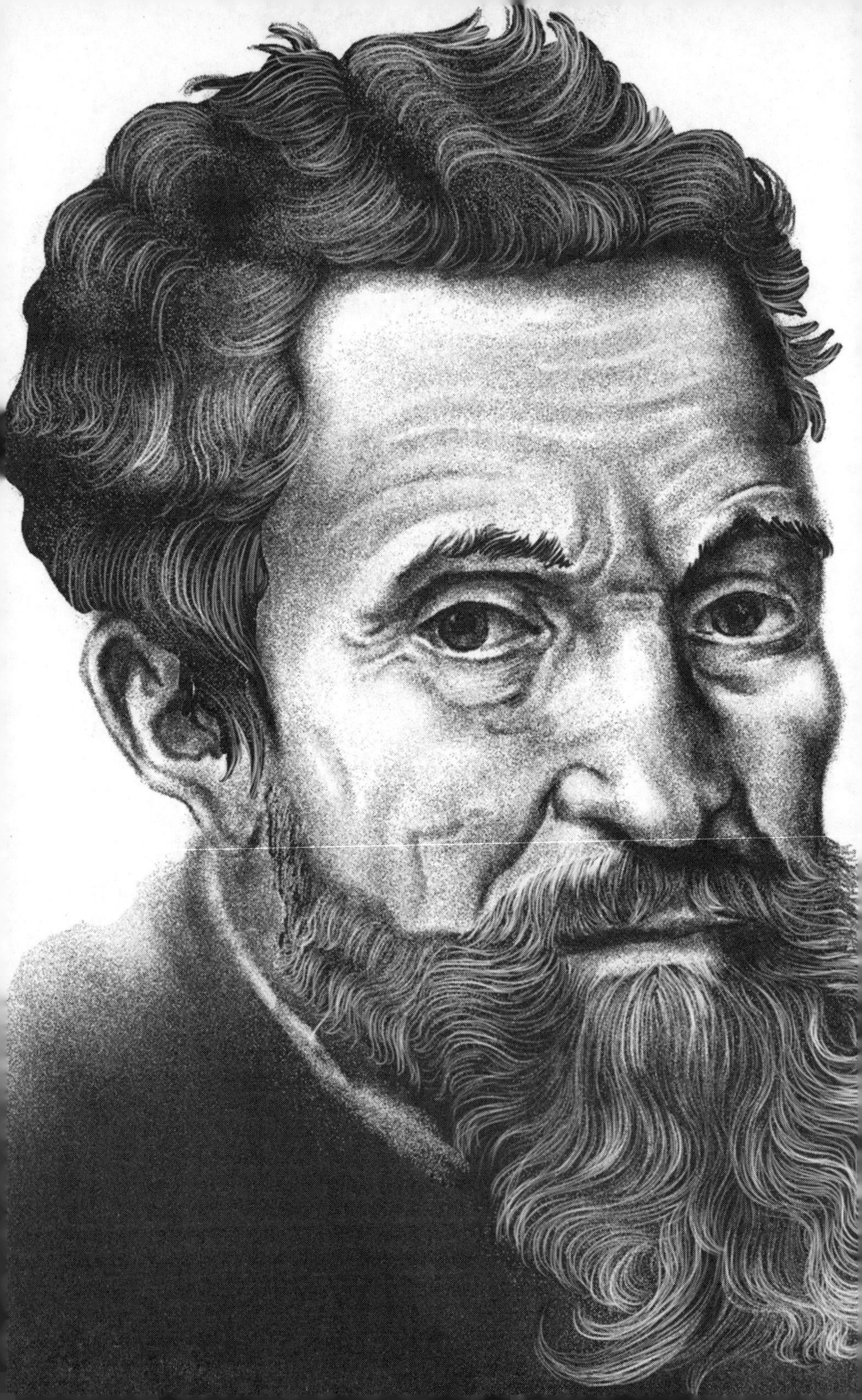

MICHELANGELO BUONAROTTI

BIRTH: *March 6, 1475*
Caprese, Italy

DEATH: *February 18, 1564 (aged 88)*
Rome, Italy

Michelangelo was an Italian Renaissance sculptor, painter, architect and poet, who was a major influence on the development of Western art. He was considered as one of the most significant artists of the High Renaissance period.

Michelangelo's full name was Michelangelo di Ludovico Buonarroti Simoni. He was born on March 6, 1475, in Italy, to Leonardo di Buonarroti Simoni. His father occasionally held goverment jobs, and at the time was the administrator of a small town called Caprese. He grew up in Florence.

Michelangelo had great interest in drawing and later, he apprenticed under the famous painter, Domenico Ghirlandaio. He decided to pursue a career in arts. He learned the technique of making frescoes. He left after one year, having nothing more to learn. Obviously talented, he was taken under the wing of the ruler of the city, Lorenzo de Medici.

Impressed by Michelangelo's work, Medici invited him to live in the Medici household. For two years, he lived with the royal Medici family. While there he met many famous poets and scholars. He worked on sculptures such as *'Madonna of the Steps'*, and *'Battle of the Centaurs'*.

He carved three statues of saints for the church. In 1495, he began his work as a sculptor. During his time in Florence, he worked on two small statues, *'St John the Baptist'* and *'Sleeping Cupid'*.

Michelangelo moved to Rome to work on

the *'Pieta'*, which was commissioned due to his *'Bacchus'*. It was one of the gems of Renaissance art. The statue showed Jesus on the lap of his mother, Mary, after Crucifixion. It was the only art that Michelangelo signed. *'Pieta'* brought Michelangelo fame, and soon he was seen as Italy's foremost sculptor.

He returned to Florence, but now as a famous artist. His next project was to carve a statue of David. It took him many years to complete this sculpture. *'David'* became Michelangelo's most popular work of art. It was seventeen feet tall and known as the largest statue made in Ancient Rome. The sculpture, considered by scholars to be nearly technically perfect, remains in Florence at the Galleria dell'Accademia.

After he completed *'David'*, he was invited back to Rome by Pope Julius II. The Pope wanted him to design his tomb. Michelangelo was commissioned to create for him a grand tomb with 40 life-sized statues. However, the Pope ended up being a fickle patron, due to the circumstances he was in, and this led to Michelangelo leaving Rome. He still continued to intermittently work on the tomb for the next several decades.

Another major project of Michelangelo's was to cover the ceiling of the Sistine Chapel with his art. It took him around four years to complete the work. The Twelve Apostles was planned as the theme. Traces of this project are seen in the 12 large figures that Michelangelo produced: seven prophets and five sibyls (female prophets) found in myths. The painting was huge and included nine scenes from the Bible. The most famous of all the scenes was *'The Creation of Adam'*. It depicted a scene in which God's hand and Adam's hand nearly touch. This was one of the most recreated scenes in the history of art, besides the *'Mona Lisa'*. He also created the *'Medici Chapel'* in Florence and the historical Laurentian Library at San Lorenzo's Church.

In 1534, he was commissioned to paint the *'The Last Judgement'* on the altar wall of the Sistine Chapel, a project he worked on for several years.

He was also a great architect. He had many talents and one of them was to design buildings.

He was a true *"Renaissance Man"*, just like Leonardo da Vinci. He even strengthened the architecture of the city of Florence. He soon became the chief architect of St Peter's Basilica in Rome. He dedicated himself to architecture and poetry during his later years.

He died on February 18, 1564 at his home in Rome, at the age of 88. He was buried in Florence. Michelangelo is considered to be one of the greatest artists of all time.

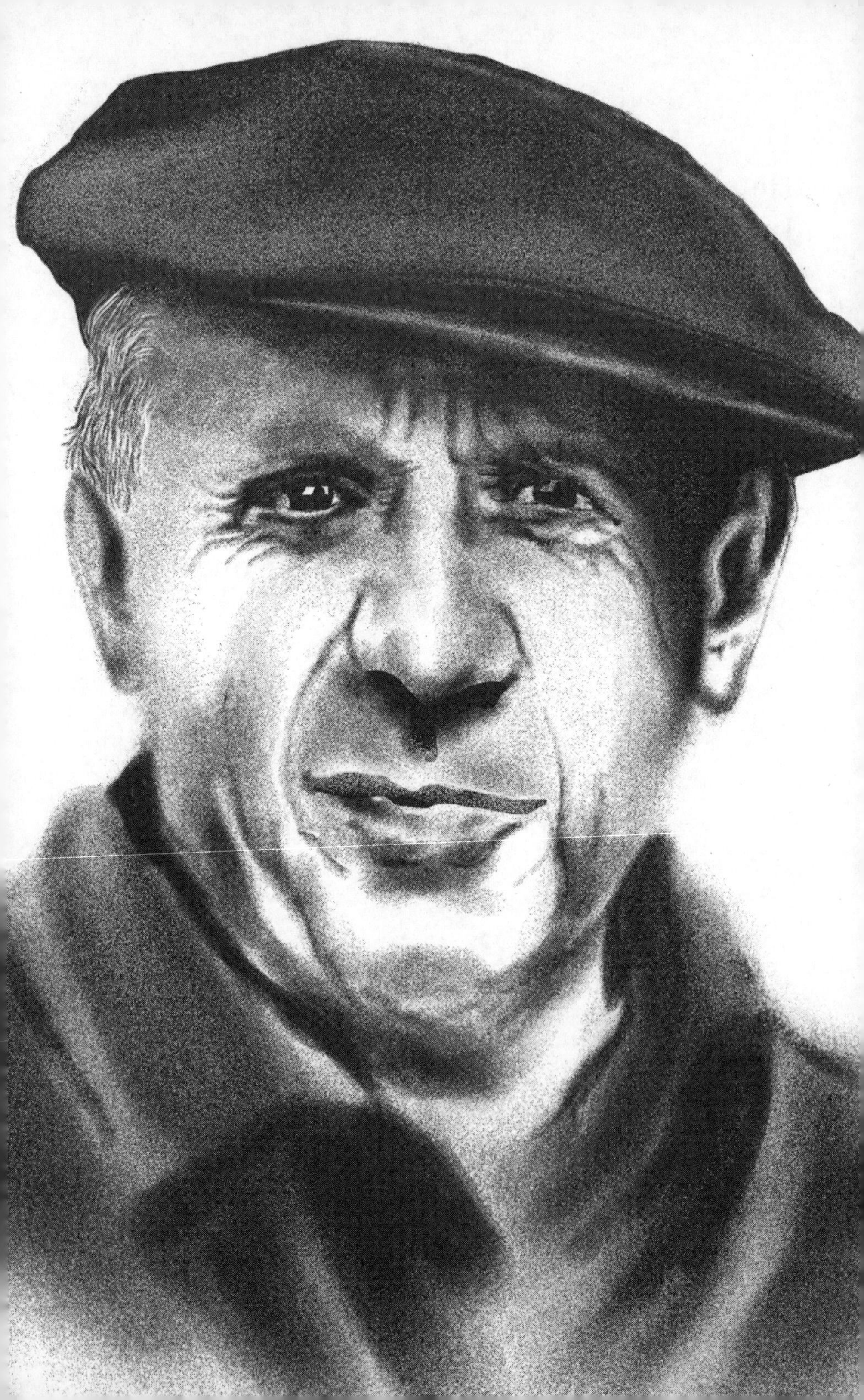

PABLO PICASSO

BIRTH: *October 25, 1881*
Málaga, Spain

DEATH: *April 8, 1973 (aged 91)*
Mougins, France

Pablo Picasso was a an expatriated Spanish painter, sculptor, printmaker and stage designer. He was one of the greatest and most prominent artists of the 20th century. He also created an art form known as "Cubism".

Pablo Picasso was born in Spain, in October 1881, to Jose Ruiz Blasco and Maria Picasso Lopez. His father was as an art professor. Picasso's artistic talent started to show early, when he became his father's pupil, at around the age of 10. In fact, his father helped Picasso hold his first exhibition at the age of 13.

Picasso's father decided to send him to the School of Fine Arts in Spain. There, he sketched whatever he observed on the streets. In 1897, he went to the Royal Academy of San Fernando. It was one of Spain's best art schools. However, he did not like what he was taught and stopped attending classes. In his spare time, he visited The Prado museum. He spent his time observing paintings by famous Spanish painters which inspired him.

At the beginning of the 20th century, he moved to Paris. He worked endlessly through the Blue period, the Rose period, Cubism, Surrealism and Realism. He mastered each of these styles and was regarded as a pioneer in each of these movements. 1901-1904 is considered to be Picasso's *"blue period"*. In the blue period, Picasso painted his art in dark colors. Most of his art was in shades of blue and blue-green. His paintings were based on the themes of poverty, anguish and melancholy. Some of his famous paintings from this era are *'Blue Nude', 'La Vie'* and *'The Old Guitarist'*.

The Rose period started around 1904. The color pink dominated much of Picasso's works.

Most of his paintings were of circus people and performers. His art was more bright and upbeat in nature. Eventually, he opened an art studio in Paris. Despite being a teenager, he had tremendous knowledge about art forms.

Picasso was also the co-creator of the art style called Cubism. He started this movement in art with his friend George Braque. Cubist art was understood, superficially, to contain abstract forms and geometric shapes. But the painters themselves believed that they were breaking the mold. Picasso dissected the visible world into abstract elements. A few of Picasso's Cubist paintings are *'Three Musicians'* and the *'Portrait of Ambroise Vollard'*.

Picasso was also a part of the Surrealist movement. The paintings made the effect of distortion on the emotions of the spectator. Picasso incorporated some Surrealism into his paintings. Some people called this time his *"Monster period"*. Examples of this art include the *'Guernica'* and *'The Red Armchair'*.

Picasso was a peace-lover. Some of the masterpieces that he created reflected this theme. His notable work of this time was the *'Guernica'* painted in 1937. Picasso painted the piece in shades of black, white and gray. It shows the tragedies of war and the suffering it inflicts upon individuals, particularly innocent civilians. This work has gained a monumental status, becoming a perpetual reminder of the tragedies of war, an anti-war symbol, and an embodiment of peace.

He eventually turned to politics during World War II and joined the French Communist Party.

He was involved in many scandals in his lifetime. However, his fans accepted him as a famous figure in the society. When the war ended, he returned to painting. He created the *'Dove of Peace'* in 1949.

Picasso is recognized as the world's most prolific painter. He created thousands of paintings and illustrations in the 78 years of his art career. He also produced various sculptures and ceramic pieces. By the time he passed away, he had produced a great collection of artworks. He influenced many aspects of cultural life as well. He even played a few roles in films, where he portrayed himself. He received many awards and honors for his skills throughout his life. He was awarded the International Lenin Peace Prize, first in 1950 and then in 1961.

Picasso married twice and had four children. He died on April 8, 1973, in Mougins, France at the age of 91. Today, Picasso is one of the most well-known artists. He dabbled in many different styles and made unique contributions to the world of art.

During his last few years, he painted self-portraits. He created his famous self-portrait with crayon on paper named '*Self-Portrait Facing Death*'. To pay tribute to this famous artist, the Museum of Modern Art, New York, dedicated its headquarters entirely to the works of one artist in a presentation.

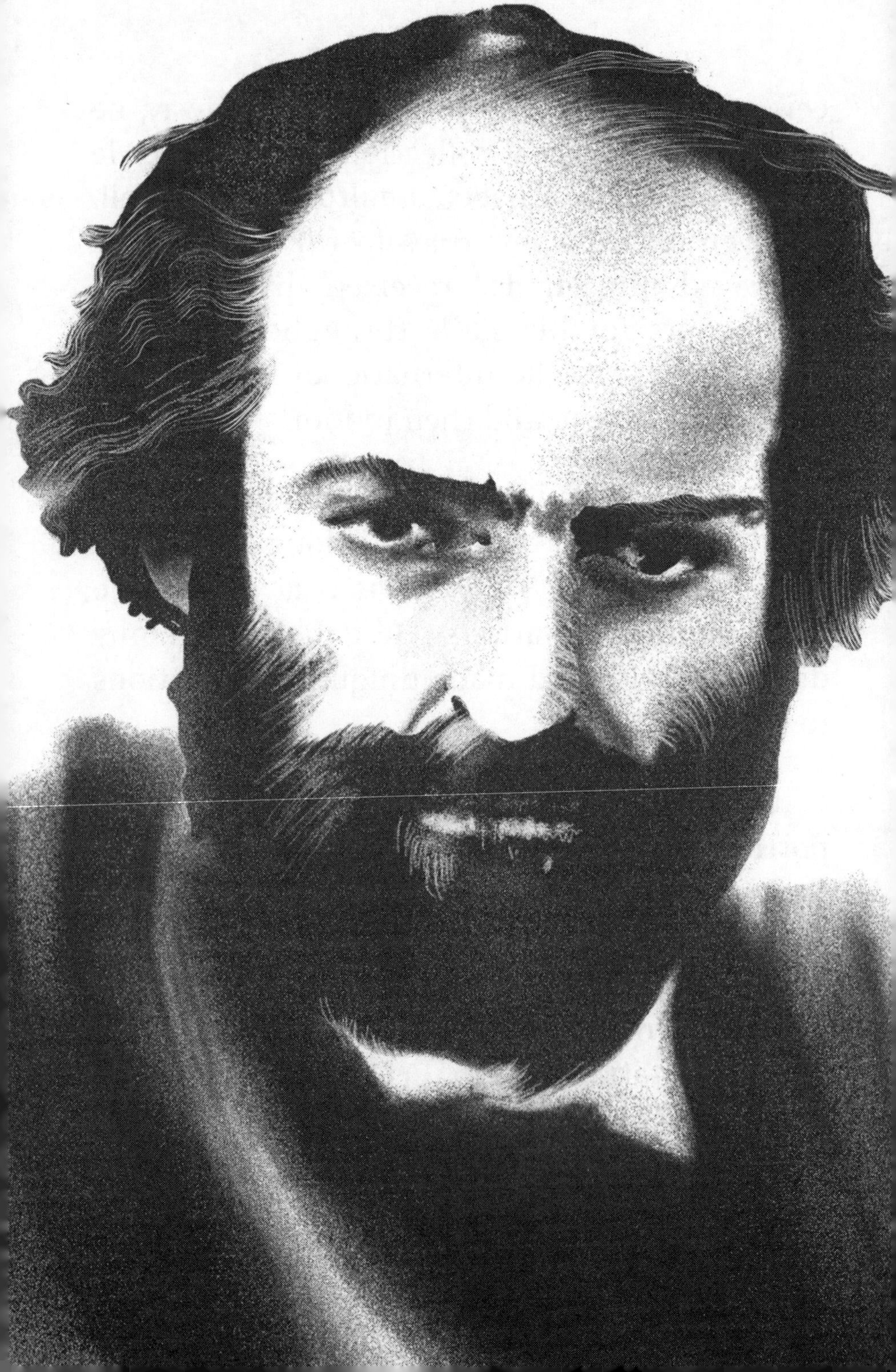

PAUL CÉZANNE

BIRTH: *January 19, 1839*
Aix, France

DEATH: *October 22, 1906 (aged 67)*
France

Paul Cézanne was one of the greatest French painters of the Post-impressionist movement. His art and ideas greatly influenced modern art. He played the role of a bridge between the late-19th century Impressionism and the early-20th century's Cubism. He is often called the "Father of Modern Art".

Paul Cézanne was born on January 19, 1839, in France to Philippe Auguste. His father owned a very successful banking firm. Thus, he belonged to a wealthy family, and Cézanne never had to worry about finances in his life. He attended Collège Bourbon in 1852. There, he met Emile Zola with whom he became great friends.

He started to take an interest in art from a very young age. His mother was the primary influence in his life. She shaped his outlook and vision towards life and art, which also showed in his work. In 1858, he studied law from the University of Aix. His father did not approve of him becoming an artist. But, Cézanne still attended drawing classes. He eventually managed to convince his father to let him go to Paris to study painting. But soon came back, after being unable to come to terms with the fact that he wasn't as technically proficient as some of the other students at Académie Suisse, where he was studying. He only managed to last for 5 months due to his friend, Zola's encouragement.

Meanwhile, he was also under massive pressure from his father, so he put his dream on hold and started to learn the family business.

After he completed his law degree, Cézanne

managed to convince his father to send him to Paris. His father sent him a small allowance every month while in Paris again. He lived there with Zola, who was already studying art in Paris. Cézanne always took an interest in the more advanced elements of the Parisian art world. He liked Romantic painters like Eugene Delacroix, Gustave Courbet and the famous Edouard Manet.

He became a well-known artist by the 1860s. His artworks were more based on heavy tones, which showcased the Romantic era. Themes like dreams, religion and more were central to his art. Cézanne used dark tones with heavy, fluid pigments for his early works.

In 1872, he practiced painting based on the Impressionist movement. Pissarro influenced most of Cézanne's works, and they even collaborated on some artwork. He also introduced him to new Impressionist techniques. Cézanne started by painting plain landscapes produced out of imagination. Nature became the key feature in Cézanne's artwork. The biggest change in his art was that he completely stopped painting religious themes. He started using more vibrant colors.

Many of his paintings were also displayed at Impressionist exhibitions. But, they were heavily criticized by the public and art critics. Due to this, he did not display his work for nearly twenty years. The painter Claude Monet also inspired his art for he painted directly from the subject, which was a characteristic of the Impressionist style. Even though he met many great painters in Paris He decided to isolate himself for a more mature style. So, he decided to go back to Aix, France and there, he painted in solitude. He also experimented with different techniques and art forms.

Some of his major works are *'Compotier'*, *'Pitcher'* and *'Fruit'* painted during 1892. They were his most famous paintings and were praised for their textures and shadows. The technique that he used revolutionized the art form in the 20th century as well.

In 1895, his art was presented to the art dealer Ambroise Vollard. During this time, his paintings became popular amongst the public. He displayed his work at the Salon for many years. Another famous piece of his was called *'Les Grandes Baigneuses'*, a masterpiece that was studied for its details and placement.

At the start of the 20th century, Cézanne became quite popular and developed a personal style. In 1904, he kept most of his artwork in a room at the Salon d'Automne allotted solely to him. The studio was known as Atelier Paul Cézanne.

Cézanne married Marie-Hortense Fiquet in 1886. She was the subject of 27 portraits painted by Cézanne, often in oil. Cézanne became ill and died on October 22, 1906, in France. To honor the great painter, the 'Cezanne Medal' was introduced by the city of Aix for achievement in the field of art.

Cubism was heavily influenced by Cézanne's short, heavy brushstrokes. His paintings, from the last three decades of his life, introduced new concepts that developed modern art.

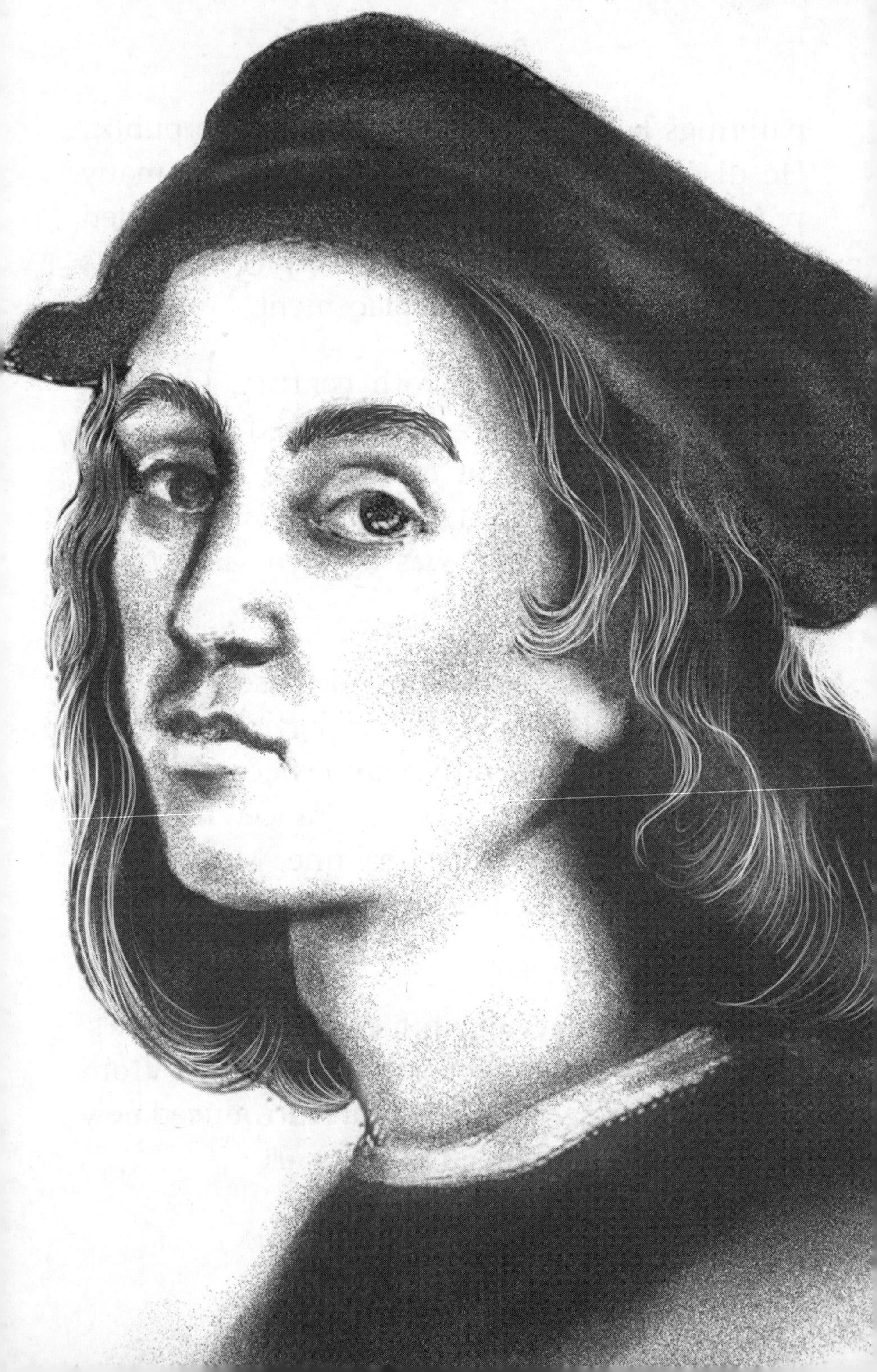

RAPHAEL

BIRTH: *April 6, 1483, Italy*

DEATH: *April 6, 1520 (aged 37)*
Rome, Italy

Raphael was an Italian painter and architect of the Italian High Renaissance. He left behind a huge collection of paintings for the world to admire. He was best-known for his works, *'Madonna'* and *'Palace of the Vatican'* in Rome.

Raphael's full name was Raffaello Sanzio. He was born on April 6, 1483, in Italy, to Giovanni Santi and Magia Ciarla. Urbino, where Raphael was born, was considered as one of the art centers of Italy, where many artists grew. His father was a painter; Raphael learned the basics of painting from him. By the age of eleven, he had lost both his parents. He was already working in his father's workshop by this time. In his uncle's care, he found an artistic foster father in Giovanni's associate, Timoteo Viti. Viti taught him initially, however, soon he realized that he himself could learn from the child. With time Raphael gained a reputation as one of the most skilled artists in Urbino. Raphael spent his significant years as a youth amongst the aristocracy, and eventually learned their ways and courtly manners. This made him popular amongst the sophisticated clients from higher classes and earned him a lot of commissions, as well as the nickname the "Prince of Painters".

Over the next few years, Raphael enhanced his artistic skills. He began to paint at an early age. He joined Pietro Perugino's workshop as a master painter at the age of 17. Because of his father's connections, Raphael was exposed to works of the Italian masters of the time. Raphael gained success early in his career. When he was in his teens, he had produced an excellent self-portrait.

He was offered to paint a large altarpiece

for the Baronci Chapel. It took him a year to complete this project. His next project was the *'Mond Crucifixion'*, an altarpiece in the Church of San Domenico. It was a painting of Jesus on the cross.

At the age of 21, he arrived in Florence. The influence of Leonardo da Vinci and Michelangelo on Florence was reflected in Raphael's work too. He grasped a lot of their style and techniques but maintained his own unique style as well. Raphael was also a charming and popular artist and many people loved his personality. He was considered a master painter and took on work from various clients including the Church. He completed three huge altarpieces, called the *'Ansidei Madonna'*, the *'Pala Baglioni'* and the *'Madonna del Baldacchino'*.

In 1508, he moved to Rome. Pope Julius II commissioned him to create a library. Raphael was also given a different room in the library to paint. *'Room of the Signatura'* was a series of frescoes painted by him in the Palace of the Vatican during this period.

It included paintings like *'The School of Athens'*, *'The Parnassus'* and *'The Disputa'*. For *'The School of Athens'*, he was recognized as one of the great artists of Italy. These paintings were based on themes like philosophy, faith, law and dramatic arts. He also painted many philosophers of Ancient Greece such as Plato, Socrates, Aristotle, Pythagoras and more.

Raphael was now in demand all over the world. During 1514, he painted *'The Mass at Bolsena'*. His next most famous painting was *'The Woman with the Veil'*. The painting was of a beautiful traditional Roman woman. Next, he painted the *'Christ Falling on the Way to Calvary'*, a work which he completed in 1517.

Soon, Raphael had set up a workshop where he taught art. Many of his students became famous artists in their own right. He designed various buildings and was considered to be one of the most important architects in Rome. In 1514, he worked on the Basilica of St Peter, chosen by Leo X. *'The Transfiguration'* was Raphael's largest painting on canvas.

Raphael never got married. He died on 6th April, 1520 in Rome, Italy at the age of 37.

With his paintings, Raphael showed variety, grace, strength and dignity. His artwork was the perfect example of Classical art and High Renaissance art. He belonged amongst the most prolific Renaissance artists and is still considered one of the greatest painters of all times.

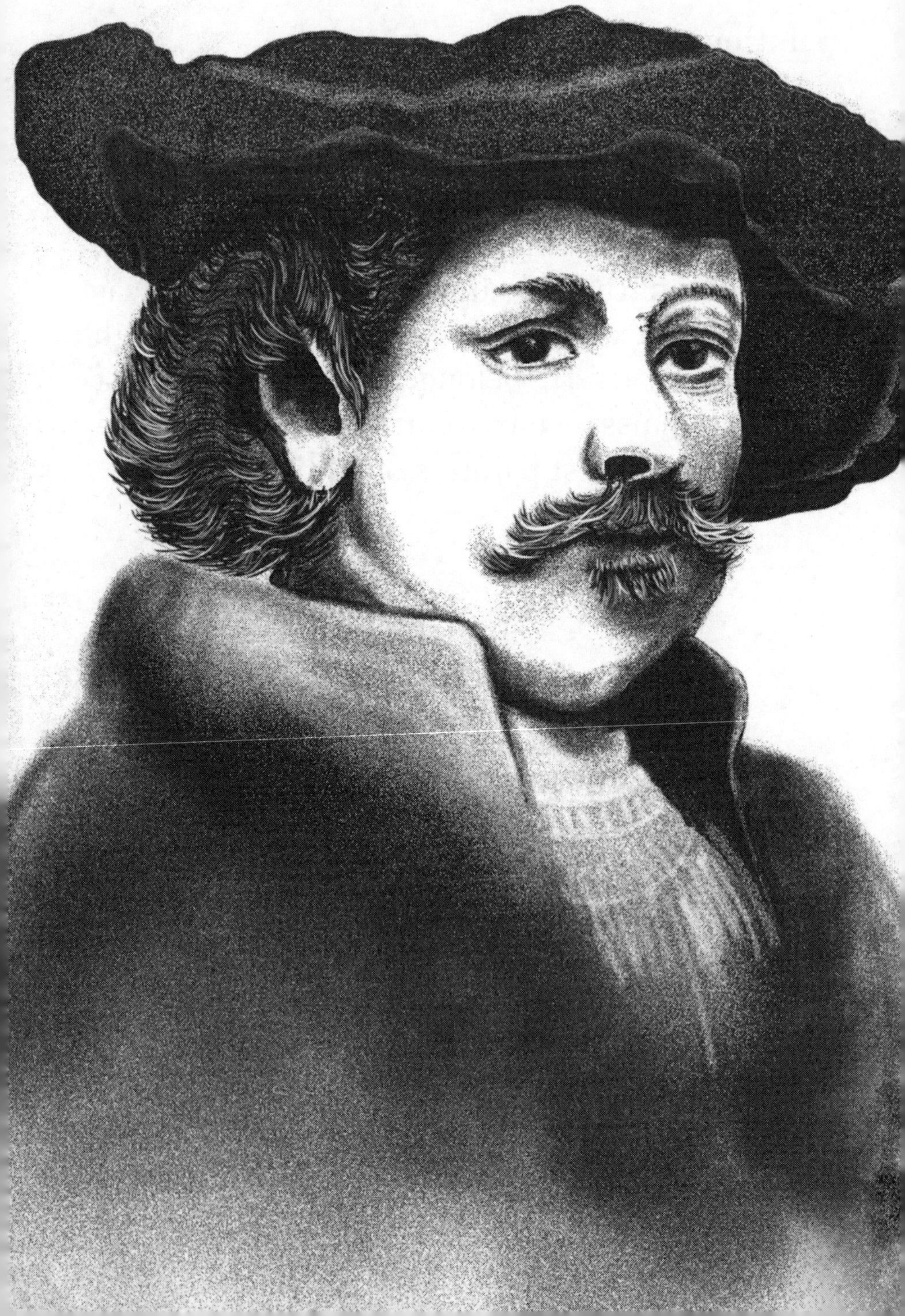

REMBRANDT

BIRTH: July 15, 1606
Leiden, Netherlands

DEATH: October 4, 1669 (aged 63)
Amsterdam, Netherlands

Rembrandt was a Dutch painter and print-maker. He was one of the greatest European painters of all times, who lived during the Dutch Golden Age. Rembrandt was most famous as a portraitist, specially remembered for his self-portraits. He was also one of the greatest storytellers in the history of art.

Rembrandt's full name was Rembrandt van Rijn. He was born on July 15, 1606, in Netherlands. He was the ninth child of his parents. His father, Harmen Gerritszoon van Rijn, was a miller.

His mother, Neeltgen Willemsdochter van Zuytbrouck, came from a family of bakers. Rembrandt received a good education and attended a Latin school as a child. Then, he went to the University of Leiden for his higher studies. But had an inclination towards painting, and knew that he wanted to learn art.

He decided to pursue art and left university. He became an apprentice under the legendary artist Jacob van Swanenburgh in 1620. He learned the basics of painting from him for the next three years. Later, he was taught art by a famous painter named Pieter Lastman.

After Rembrandt completed his training, he became a professional artist. Soon, he returned to Leiden as a master, and probably moved into a studio along with a fellow pupil of Lastman's, Jan Lievens. At the age of twenty-one, he started to teach others how to paint. By the end of his life, he'd taught the most well-known artists during his time.

Rembrandt started experimenting with painting biblical scenes. Portraits of people and their families were a trend in Amsterdam at the time. So, by 1631, he had many prominent Amsterdam residents commissioning portraits, and by 1632 he moved to the city, and practiced as a professional portraitist for the first time, eventually gaining a reputation as a famous portrait artist.

Rembrandt also painted many self-portraits and pictures of his own family members. His paintings were special in their own way. He captured a person's personality and emotion on the canvas. He also used light and shadow to create a mood. His energetic works gained him numerous commissions. He painted many influential people including the Prince. He developed his own art style, in which he painted by using light and illumination. Some of his paintings like *'Peter and Paul Disputing'*, and *'Returning the Pieces of Silver'* were based on the concept of light.

Rembrandt met statesman Huygens, who proved to be a useful acquaintance for the artist. Huygens often appreciated Rembrandt's paintings and even helped the artist sell paintings to the court of The Hague. For the next few years, Rembrandt stayed with an art dealer named Hendrick Uylenburgh. Hendrick was the owner of a workshop who created portraits and restored paintings. With Hendrick, Rembrandt met many who commissioned him for their portraits.

Rembrandt also enjoyed painting dramatic, biblical and mythological scenes in high contrast and a large format. Some such works were *'The Rising of Lazarus'*, *'The Return of the Prodigal Son'* and *'The Visitation'*. Later, he began to paint landscapes which highlighted drama. He used to draw uprooted trees and gloomy skies in his landscapes. Some of his landscape paintings are the *'Winter Scene'*, *'Landscape with a Stony Bridge'* and *'Stormy Landscape'*. He painted them on a large canvas and it took him days to finish one painting.

During 1640, his paintings became less playful and more serious in tone. Biblical pictures were now derived more often from the New Testament than the Old Testament. Another one of Rembrandt's masterpieces was called *'The Night Watch'*. His most famous work was a large portrait of Captain Banning Cocq and his military men. He painted each man a little differently so it looked more like a giant action scene. He used his famous light and shadow technique for this project.

Another important work of his was the painting *'The Anatomy Lesson of Dr Nicolaes Tulp'*. It became a much-discussed piece in the medical world. It was an oil painting in which he'd portrayed the famous Dutch surgeon.

Rembrandt married Saskia van Uylenburgh in 1634. His family life was marked by many personal tragedies, which he also depicted in his paintings. His wife died young which left him devastated.

Rembrandt earned a lot of money from his art projects throughout his career and thus owned a large house. However, in 1657 it was sold along with his other possessions. He died on 4th October, 1669 in Amsterdam. Rembrandt is considered to be one of the greatest artists in the history of art and the most significant Dutch painter of all times.

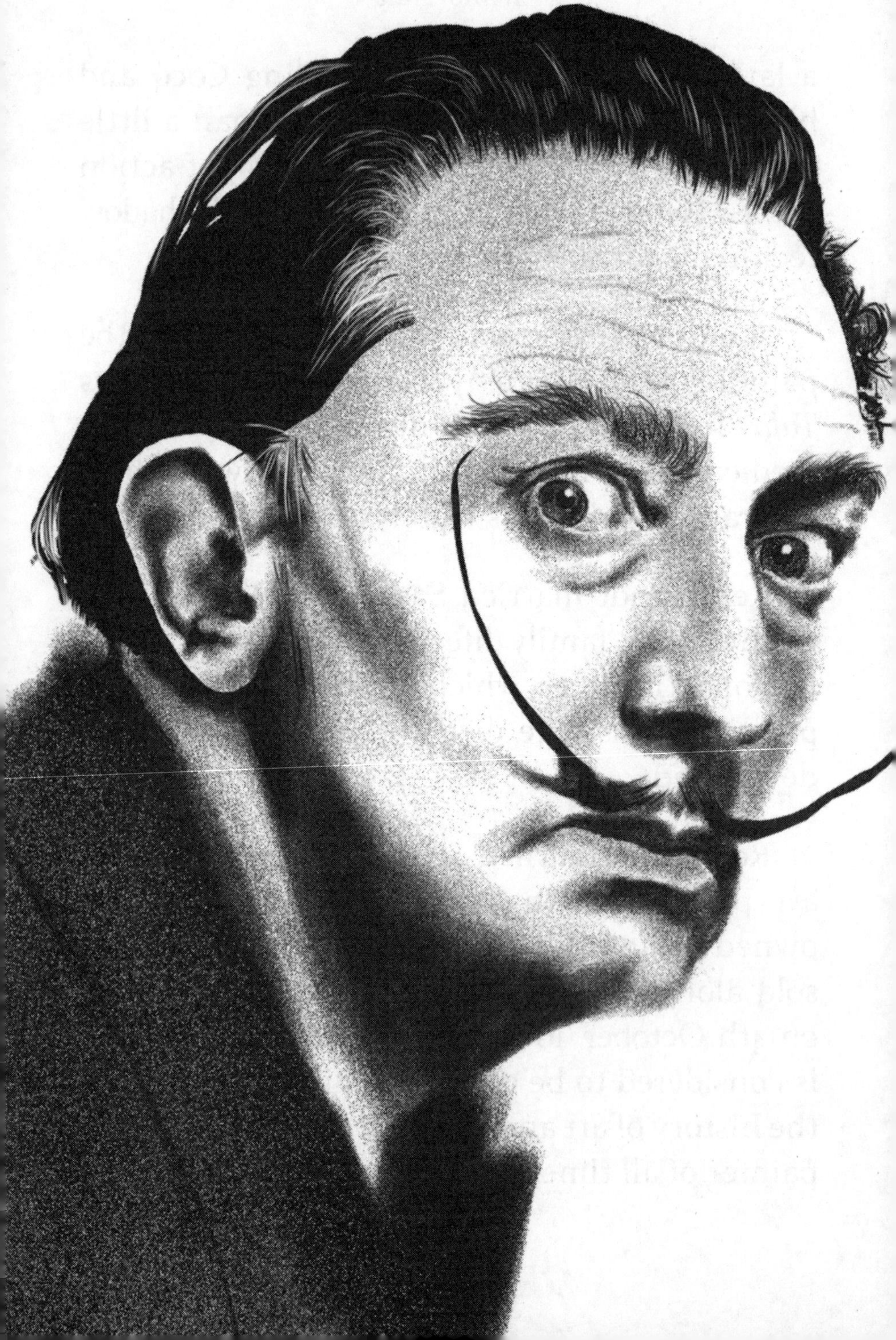

SALVADOR DALI

BIRTH: *May 11, 1904*
Figueres, Spain

DEATH: *January 23, 1989*
Figueres, Spain

Salvador Dali was one of the most talented and prolific artists of the 20th century. He was known for innovations and advances in a new art genre called Surrealism. Dali took inspiration from the thoughts, ideas and artworks of the Renaissance period.

Dali's real name was Salvador Felipe Jacinto Dalí y Domenech. He was born on 11th May, 1904 in Catalonia, Spain to Salvador Dali I Cusi and Felipa Domenech Ferres. He had one sister and a brother who died at a young age. His father was a notary and his mother loved art. As a kid, he developed an interest in painting and football.

Dali started painting at a very young age and went to an art school. He painted outdoor scenes of sailboats and houses. He also did portraits. As a teenager, he experimented with different painting styles including Impressionism. In 1922, he moved to Spain and attended the Academy of Fine Arts. There, he learned the skills and techniques which he later used in his paintings. In his college days, he behaved in a rebellious way, which led him into trouble.

Dali had always had a creative streak. After he graduated from art school, he began to experiment with different art styles.

Dali explored Classic art, Cubism, Surrealism, and more. First, he concentrated on Cubist art. Pichot educated him more about this art form. He learned Cubist art from magazines, articles and catalogs. There was no cubist artist around him at the time.

In 1924, he completed his first illustrated book. He got expelled from his art college, but continued to create art regardless. In 1926, he created his famous artwork, *'Basket of Bread'*. The same year, he moved to Paris. He met Pablo Picasso, who was a pioneer of Cubism. Dali had always admired Picasso's art. Most of Dali's works carried heavy influences of Picasso. With him, Dali developed his own art style.

He then got interested in Surrealism. Surrealism was first started by the French poet Andre Breton. The word "surrealism" means "above realism". He learned this art form from artists like Rene Magritte and Joan Miro. He spent most of his time working on Surrealist art. Soon, he became one of the dominant artists of the Surrealist movement. He also grew a thin mustache that curved up at either end. His mustache became his trademark.

'The Persistence of Memory' became Dali's most famous painting. It was his most significant contribution to the Surrealist movement. It was a natural looking desert landscape covered with melting watches. His next painting, also on the Surrealism theme, was *'Swans*

Reflecting Elephants'.

He used reflections in his other artworks as well like in *'Metamorphosis of Narcissus'*. The painting told the story of a man named Narcissus.

Dali made many sculptures and also contributed to theatre, fashion, and photography, which were amongst his other areas of interest. He created jewels which involved beautiful artwork. The most famous one was *'The Royal Heart'*. Dali also assisted the Surrealist film director Luis Bunuel. They released a short film called *An Andalusian Dog*. He worked on the Disney short film *Destino* as well. He released another film called *Moontide* in 1942. He was also known as a great author. He released his autobiography called *The Secret Life of Salvador Dali* (also in 1942) and a novel about automobiles.

Around World War II, Dali moved to the United States. He gained international recognition as many of his artworks portrayed the horrors of the World War. Later on, his focus shifted to religion. He painted much artwork about religion. One of his famous paintings during this time was the *'Christ of St John of the Cross'*. The painting showed a cross floating high in the sky and a lake with a boat and some fishermen.

Dali married Gala in 1934. Gala's death left him devastated. He died on 23rd January, 1989 in Spain because of heart failure. Today, Dali's art inspires many young artists.

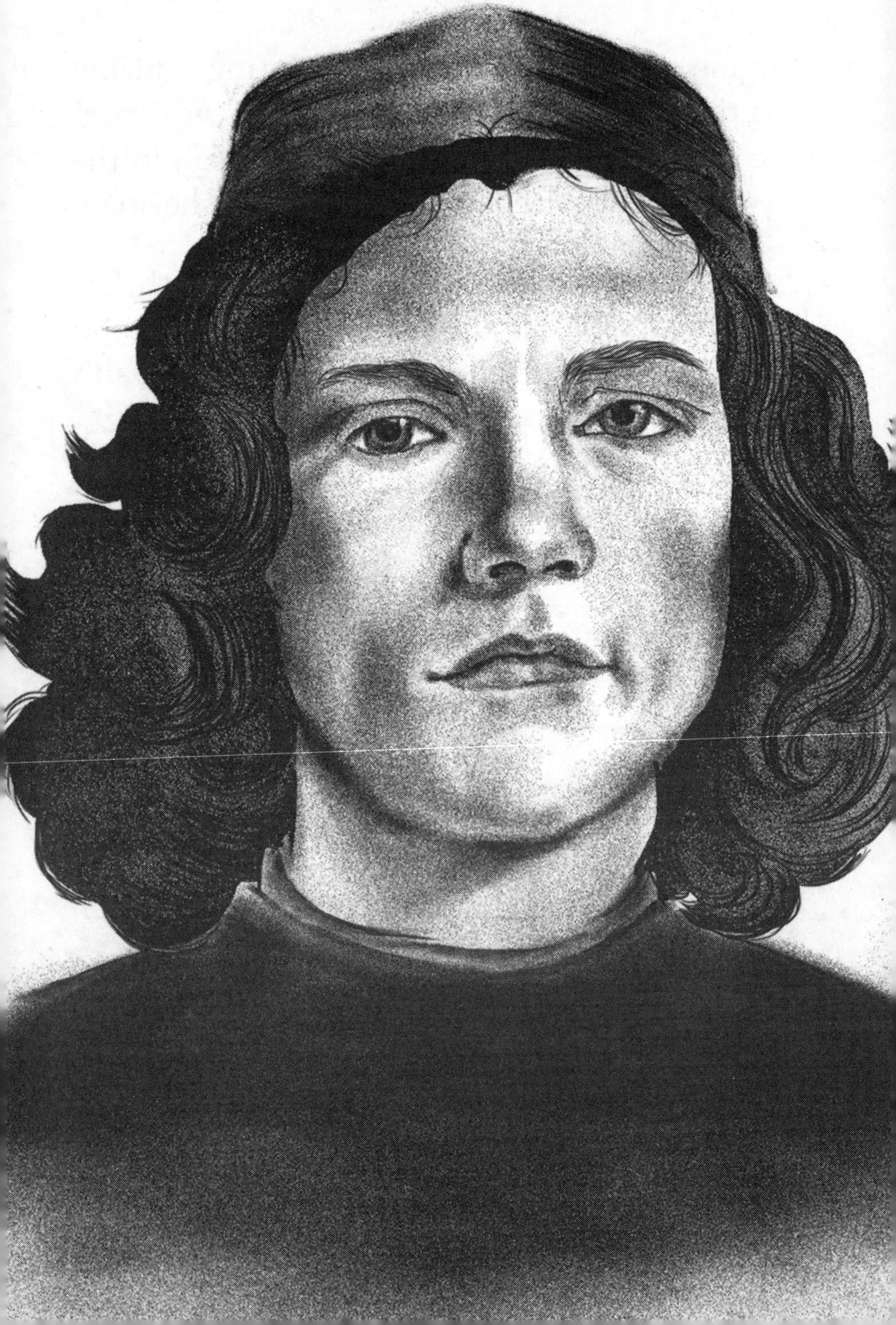

SANDRO BOTTICELLI

❧❦❧

BIRTH: 1445, Florence, Italy

DEATH: May 17, 1510 (aged 65)
Florence, Italy

Sandro Botticelli was one of the greatest painters of the Renaissance. His major works include *'The Birth of Venus'* and *'Primavera'*. He was one of the great painters of the Italian Renaissance, a period that witnessed the revival of Roman and Greek culture in Italy.

Sandro Botticelli's real name was Alessandro di Mariano Filipepi. He was born in 1445 in Florence to Mariano di Filipepi. Most of Botticelli's personal life was scattered, but his professional career is well documented. At first, he was trained to become a goldsmith. His father apprenticed him under a goldsmith before realizing that Botticelli's interest lay in art. He then joined Filippo Lippi, an admired Florentine master, as an apprentice.

He completed his entire education under the guidance of Lippi. Most of Botticelli's artworks were influenced by the elder master.

He adopted Lippi's specific technique. His paintings were lifelike and three-dimensional. By the time he was 25, he owned a workshop.

Botticelli was also greatly influenced by Andrea del Verrocchio, where Leonardo da Vinci worked. Later in his life, Botticelli met Lorenzo de Medici, another great artist. Medici used his talent and encouraged him to explore new art styles. Botticelli used circular *'Tondo'* forms, which were circular paintings. He painted beautiful female portraits and human figures, which dominated his earliest works. Some of his paintings on panels were *'Madonna with Child'*, *'Portrait of a Young Man'*, *'Fortitude'* and

'St Sebastian'.

In 1475, he painted the *'Adoration of the Magi'*, which featured a portrait of Lorenzo de Medici's grandfather. It was one of his masterpieces. His other works include *'The Birth of Christ'* and *'St Augustine'*. In 1481, he was asked to paint the walls of the Sistine Chapel by Pope Sixtus IV. It took him two years to complete the work. He made four paintings including *'St Sixtus II'*, *'Punishment of Korah Dathan and Abiram'*, *'The Temptation of Christ'* and *'The Trials of Moses'*.

Botticelli's two masterpieces were painted for the Villa of Lorenzo Medici at Castello in the mid-16th century. He painted the *'Primavera'* in 1478 and *'The Birth of Venus'* in 1485. Both his works were influenced by Humanism. These paintings earned global recognition from scholars for many years.

Post-1490, Botticelli's paintings had a new art style. He started painting smaller figures on the canvas. Some of these works are *'Calumny of Apelles'*, *'The Last Communion of St Jerome'*, *'The Descent of the Holy Ghost'*, *'Madonna and Child'* and *'Angel'*. This style became more famous because of the dreamy look of the people in his paintings; the characters looked more lively.

Botticelli's art was also profoundly influenced by religion. One such painting based on this theme was the *'Adoration of the Magi'*. It was a painting of Mary and the baby Jesus. Botticelli even portrayed himself in a brown robe in that piece. He became a follower of Girolamo Savonarola, a Dominican preacher. Botticelli then painted the *'The Mystical Nativity'*. Botticelli also painted mythological scenes in his artworks like the *'Birth of Venus'*, in which he painted Venus, the Roman Goddess of love and beauty.

His later works were a series of paintings which represented the life-cycle of St. Zenobius. Two of these paintings were the *'Four Scenes from the Early Life of Saint Zenobius'* in 1500 and *'Three Miracles of St. Zenobius'* in 1505. Botticelli did not paint much in his old age. He became disabled, which resulted in a lack of projects. During the period of High Renaissance, his art was shadowed by the fresh styles of Michelangelo and Leonardo da Vinci.

Botticelli remained unmarried all his life. He died on May 17, 1510 at the age of 65 in Florence, Italy. After the death of the great painter, most of his paintings were left undisturbed. None of his works were moved from the churches or homes.

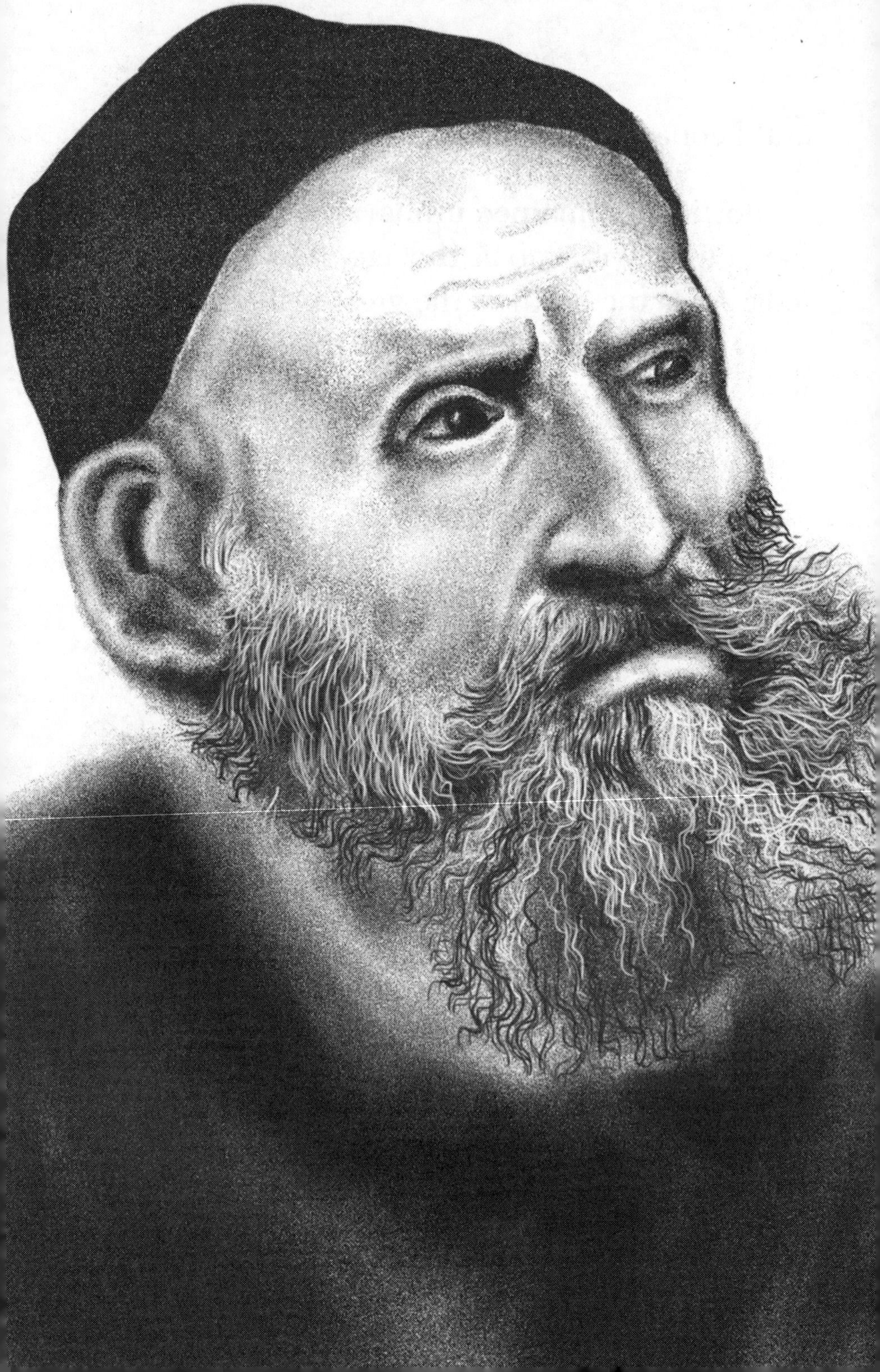

TITIAN

BIRTH: c. 1488
Pieve di Cadore, Italy

DEATH: August 27, 1576
Venice, Italy

Titian was an Italian painter and one of the greatest artists of the Renaissance period. Titian painted artworks for royals such as King Philip II, Pope Paul III and the Holy Roman Emperor Charles V. He was recognized as a great painter of his era.

Titian's full name was Tiziano Vecellio. He was born between 1488 and 1490, near Pieve di Cadore, in Italy to Gregorio Vecellio and Lucia. His father was a modest official. His family was well-established in the area. Titian was 9 years old when he was sent to live with his uncle in Venice. He lived there for many years. He soon developed an interest in painting and decided to pursue a career as an artist.

Titan and his brother were trained as painters by the famous artist Sebastiano Zuccato. He met many skilled artists such as Giovanni Bellini and Giorgione, who influenced him. Titian's brother stayed in Venice and continued his studies there. But, Titian left the city and began a collaboration with Giorgione. Most of his works were inspired by Giorgione, and his teacher at school, Bellini. Their styles were very similar, and no one could tell the difference between their paintings. His early works included *'The Meeting at the Golden Gate'* and *'The Miracle of the Jealous Husband'*.

He soon gained the attention of buyers. His first major commission from St Anthony of Padua came in 1510. He began his own workshop and painted some religious works like *'Gypsy Madonna'* and *'The Madonna of the Cherries'*. These works were famous for the colors that Titian used in his artwork. As an artist, he also became an interpreter of mythology. He created some important works like *'Flora'* and *'Sacred and Profane Love'*. 1516 to 1530 were the years when Titian showed his mastery and maturity as an artist. Titian moved on from his earlier style and tackled larger and more complex subjects. He attempted a monumental style.

During 1516, he was offered another project. He had to paint the high altar in the Church of Maria Gloriosa in Venice. He created one of the masterpieces called *'The Assumption of the Virgin for the Church'*. The painting skilfully used vivid colors and beautifully showed the human forms. This art established him as one of the leading painters of the era in Venice. It brought him honor and glory throughout the Renaissance.

After he finished his last painting, he was commissioned by the Duke of Ferrara, Alfonso d'Este. He painted some mythological artworks like *'Worship of Venus'*, *'Bacchus and Ariadne'*, and *'The Bacchanal of the Andrians'*. Most of his works were based on religious themes. He painted them in oil-paint, which was an innovative technique that time. His next work was '*Martyrdom of St Peter Martyr*'. In 1522, he created '*A Man with a Glove*', which was a portrait of a wealthy man.

Titian never learned to engrave, but he knew the importance of printmaking. He wanted to expand his body of work further. In 1520, he designed some woodcuts. One of them was a large and impressive one called '*The Crossing of the Red Sea*'.

During 1530, Charles V showed his appreciation of the artist's precocity by making him a knight of the Golden Spur and Count Palatine. He painted his first portrait of Charles V when he attended the coronation of the Emperor. In 1538, he painted '*Venus of Urbino*'. This artwork was based on Giorgione's art style. This painting became an inspiration for other painters as well. Titian visited Rome at the request of Pope Paul III. There, he saw the Renaissance works of great painters such as Raphael and Michelangelo. He also painted many masterpieces like '*Paul III and his Grandsons*' during this time.

In Venice, he continued to produce art like the *'Christ Crowned with Thorns'* and *'Martyrdom of St Lawrence'*. In 1550, Titian painted a portrait of Prince Philip in armor. It set an example for state portraits.

Titian married Cecilia Soldani and the couple had three children. Titian died of plague on August 27, 1576 in Venice. The home that he lived in was raided by thieves, due to which most of Titian's possessions were gone.

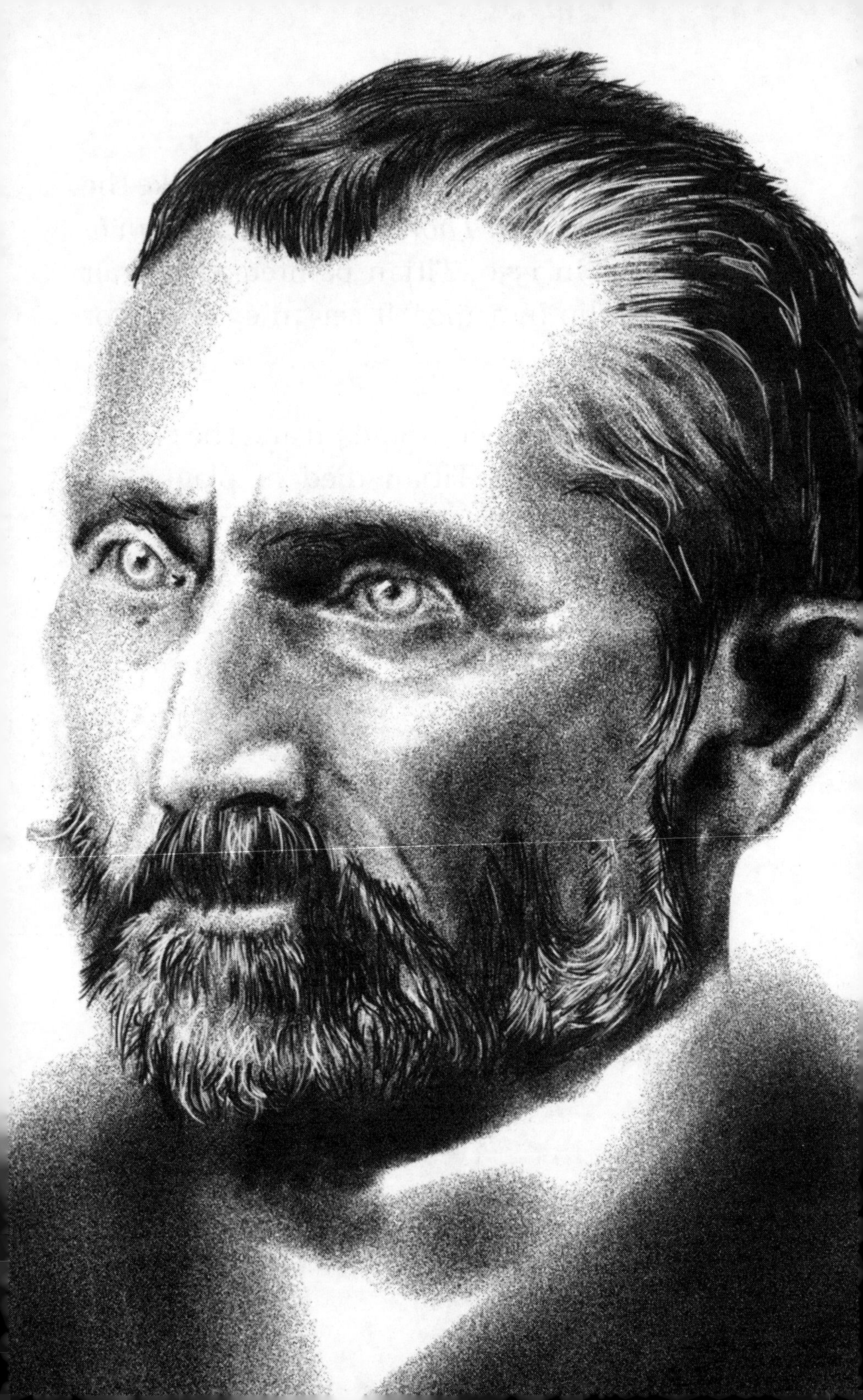

VINCENT VAN GOGH

❦

BIRTH: *March 30, 1853*
Zundert, Netherlands

DEATH: *July 29, 1890 (aged 37)*
Auvers-sur-Oise, France

Vincent van Gogh was a Dutch artist. An incredibly famous painter, his expensive works now crown museums and collections across the world.

Vincent Willem van Gogh was born on March 30, 1853 in the Netherlands to Theodorus van Gogh and Anna Cornelia Carbentus. He had five siblings, and Gogh was most fond of his brother, Theo. His father was a minister.

His mother was an artist and her love for art was transferred to her son. Van Gogh took an interest in art from a very young age and, as an occupation, it came naturally to him. He was intelligent and excelled in languages at school.

Van Gogh's uncle got him a job at an art dealership in The Hague. After he finished his training, he joined Messrs Goupil & Co., serving them first at the branch at the Hague, and then in London. He had the most productive years of his early art career in London. He mastered French, German and the English language. He fell in love with English culture. In 1873, he worked briefly in the Goupil Gallery.

Van Gogh used to read the writings of affluent writers like Charles Dickens and George Eliot. At the age of 27, he decided to pursue a career as an artist. He was accepted into the Royal Academy of Art in Brussels. He learned the basics and the theory of art there.

Van Gogh started drawing pictures using pencils and charcoal sticks. Finally, he began to paint using oil paints. At the beginning of his career, he used a lot of dark colors. Most of his art appeared gloomy or sad. He liked to draw pictures of people. During 1885, he began work on his first masterpiece. It was called *'The Potato Eaters'.* It was a picture of a farmer family eating potatoes for dinner. His younger brother Theo was an art dealer and tried selling Vincent's paintings, but no one bought them.

Then, Van Gogh moved to Paris where he dabbled in a new art style. Theo told him about a new style of painting called Impressionism. It had soon become a dominant art form in Paris. He too was inspired by the same.

Van Gogh soon became interested in bright colors. His brushwork also became more broken. He painted the streets, people and cafes of Paris. He would sometimes paint himself for practice. He painted over twenty self-portraits in this time.

In 1888, Van Gogh moved to France and started an artist community. He became a good friend of the artist Paul Gauguin. He painted local landscapes and loved to replicate the vibrant colors of the bright sun of France. He would apply the paint directly onto the canvas from the tubes leaving the paint thick. His paintings became more and more bright and colorful. Van Gogh painted hundreds of pictures, sometimes in a single day. He became thoroughly engrossed in art. He painted some of the most famous paintings like *'Van Gogh's Chair'*, *'Bedroom in Arles'*, *'The Night Cafe'*, *'Cafe Terrace at Night'* and *'Starry Night Over the Rhone'*.

Van Gogh used to spend more of his money on paint than on food. His health started to deteriorate and he faced a lot of mental issues. Gauguin and Van Gogh had become very close friends by this time. They would spend their day painting. Van Gogh painted *'The Red Vineyard'* for Gauguin. Gauguin painted Van Gogh's portrait of *'The Painters of Sunflower'*. However, their friendship started to get affected as they fought very often. Later in life, his mental health declined further. In the hospital, Van Gogh spent his days painting. During his stay, he began painting the clinic and the hospital garden which became the main subject of his drawings. He painted the masterpieces, *'The Starry Night'*, *'Olive Trees with the Alpilles in the Background'*, *'Cornfield with Cypresses'* and *'Country road in Provence by Night'*. The common elements in all of these were the cypress trees and a lot of swirling colors.

Many of Van Gogh's romantic relationships failed throughout his life. He died on July 29, 1890 at the age of 37 in France.

Van Gogh left a great legacy behind. He was not entirely appreciated during his lifetime and sold only one painting during the entirety of his art career. However, today he is considered to be one of the greatest artists of all time.

QUESTIONS

Q.1. Andy Warhol sketched the picture of which famous communist leader?

Q.2. *'The Cathedrals of France'* was made by which painter?

Q.3. Who is considered to be the founder of Impressionism?

Q.4. Which is Edvard Munch's most famous painting?

Q.5. What is Pointillism?

Q.6. Who created Cubism?

Q.7. Henri Matisse was a member of which movement?

Q.8. Which year did Turner create his first oil painting in?

Q.9. Which artist painted *'The Girl with a Pearl Earring'*?

Q.10. Which artist is known as *'The Father of Modern Art'*?

Q.11. What type of artwork is Frida Kahlo best known for?

Q.12. Name the different art movements and styles which Pablo Picasso mastered.

Q.13. What are the Rose and Blue periods?

Q.14. Pablo Picasso's *'Guernica'* was painted using which three colors?

Q.15. Which painting did Gustav Klimt create in the golden phase?

Q.16. What is the name of Gustave Klimt's most famous painting?

Q.17. Whose ceiling did Michelangelo cover with art? Which famous scene did he create?

Q.18. Who lived during the Dutch Golden Age era?

Q.19. What is the Fauvist movement?

Q.20. For which building did Henry Matisse design the interiors and glass windows?

Q.21. What art technique did Johannes Vermeer use in his works?

Q.22. Whose portraits did Titian create as a royal

court painter?

Q.23. Paul Cezanne was part of which two movements?

Q.24. Who is best known for the Abstract Expressionism movement?

Q.25. Who traveled with King Louis-Philippe to Morocco?

Q.26. Which famous art technique did Rembrandt use for his projects?

Q.27. Name J.M.W. Turner's well-known paintings.

Q.28. What are the significant mythological art-works that Titian made?

Q.29. Who was the creator of 'Christ of St. John of the Cross'?

Q.30. What is the name of Salvador Dali's Disney short film?

DID YOU KNOW?

1. Leonardo da Vinci was ambidextrous, which means he was able to use the right and left hands equally well. But he painted with his right hand.

2. Pablo Picasso was fascinated with the mythical creature 'Minotaur', which had the body of a man and the head of a bull. It appeared in many of his paintings.

3. No two of the 300 people painted on the ceiling of the Sistine Chapel by Michelangelo look alike.

4. Claude Monet once said, "Everyone discusses my art and pretends to understand as if it were necessary to understand when it is simply necessary to love."

5. Georges Seurat painted art in dots which were like pixels on a computer screen.

6. Henri Matisse ran an art school called Academie 'Matisse in Paris'.

7. J. M. W. Turner liked traveling to Venice which inspired a number of his paintings.

8. Leonardo da Vinci wrote everything as mirror image so that others couldn't copy his works.

9. Raphael was often viewed as a rival to Michelangelo.

10. All the watches painted in Salvador Dali's *'The Persistence of Memory'* tell different times.

11. Vincent van Gogh was influenced by Japanese prints and woodcuts, and studied them intently.

12. Picasso's paintings have been sold for over a $100 million.

13. As a child, Edouard Manet loved to go to the Louvre museum.

14. Henri Matisse was good friends with the artist Pablo Picasso, but later they became rivals.

15. Rembrandt's home in Amsterdam was turned into the Rembrandt House Museum.